TABLE OF CONTENTS

FINDING CAPTAIN MYLES STANDISH

2020 - We too are descendants of Myles Standish Sandy's son, Steve Hall has proof!

Ch 1	Forward	1–3		Ch 14	The General Sickness	77–80
Ch 2	Spices, Furs, Adventure	4–6		Ch 15	Pilgrim Hall, Duxbury	81–86
Ch 3	One Man Army	7–10		Ch 16	Plimouth Plantation	87–89
Ch 4	Monstrous Innovations	11–15		Ch 17	Samoset and Squanto	90–95
Ch 5	Excessive Jollity	16–21		Ch 18	Treaty with Massasoit	96–101
Ch 6	Good-natured and Very Fat	22–27		Ch 19	Standish Monument	102–108
Ch 7	As I Remember It	28–33		Ch 20	Ashfield, Mass.	109–111
Ch 8	Loathe to Depart	34–38		Ch 21	Baptist Corners	112–118
Ch 9	Olde Ponde Place	39–46		Ch 22	Finding Amie and Submit	119–125
Ch 10	The Crossing	47–54		Ch 23	Genealogic Jig Saw	126–128
Ch 11	The First Expeditions	55–60		Ch 24	Standish-Young Lineage	129–133
Ch 12	The First Encounter	61–69		Ch 25	Frequently Asked Question	134–137
Ch 13	Moving Ashore	70–76		Ch 26	Bibliography	138–140

Acknowledgement

As anyone who has ever attempted to write a book soon discovers, the first few drafts are the easy part; getting it letter perfect and typo free is an entirely different matter. I am grateful to my dear wife Ruth and daughters Tory and Barbara who, along with special friends Alice and George, massaged my often-tangled prose and patiently corrected my all-too-frequent misspellings. ~ RHH

---

*Husband of Ruth Harms '52 classmate ETHS
Friend of Alice Butler '52
my dear friend gave me this book!*

Chapter One

FINDING CAPTAIN MYLES STANDISH

Forward

Standish gravestone, Duxbury

The title of this book may be a bit misleading; the venerable Captain is not at all hard to find. His remains repose in a well-marked grave in Duxbury, the town he and John Alden founded just across the bay from Plymouth Colony. However, calling this book, "Proving Descent from Captain Myles Standish and Retracing in Reverse the Westward Migration of His Descendants" seems a bit cumbersome.

I first became aware of a possible Standish connection back in 1944, when I stayed with Grandmother Victoria Young Haviland during my freshman year in high school. Each evening when chores were finished and dishes done, Tory would spin tales of her younger days, some of them obviously embellished to make them all the more interesting. One such story was that she and, therefore, her children and their progeny, descended from the renowned military leader of the Mayflower Pilgrims, Captain Myles Standish. But, when pressed for details, Tory could provide no specifics other than to say that her father, Calvin Young, had a brother named Standish. This was far from convincing at the time but it stuck in my mind and, nearly fifty years later, provided one of the clues that helped to convince me to try to prove or disprove her claim.

Tory passed away in 1956 at age 79, and with her gone, the "Standish issue" gave way to other, more pressing personal priorities but it was not forgotten. Sporadically, over the next several decades I contacted various county vital record keepers in Wisconsin, Michigan and Pennsylvania, gradually building up a limited file of great grandparents—who they were, where and when they lived, etc. I had yet to find any Standishes but it began to appear at least possible that the family lore about Myles was worthy of further investigation.

Chapter One

FINDING CAPTAIN MYLES STANDISH

Forward

Then, thanks to Walter Young of Elkhart, Indiana—more about him later—I became aware of the name of my great-great grandfather, Alonzo Young of Amity Township in Erie County, Pennsylvania. Calvin, one of Alonzo's sons, was Victoria's father and I was especially pleased to find that another of Alonzo's sons was named Standish, proving that Tory was, at the very least, right about this much. But, just where Alonzo was born and the names of his parents could not be determined from Erie County records, indicating he was born elsewhere, but where?

Not knowing where to look next, I telephoned the venerable Mayflower Society in Plymouth. Although they did not provide genealogical research services, they referred me to the Pilgrim Society in nearby Duxbury where they would be better able to assist me.

I called them, informed them of our long-standing family lore concerning Captain Myles Standish, and requested help in proving or disproving its accuracy. I was surprised and delighted to receive an immediate reply from Elaine Corbett, who identified herself as a volunteer researcher at the Pilgrim Museum. She explained that she was particularly interested in working with Standish and Alden descendants and that there would be no charge for these services, welcome news, indeed.

Contrary to what is commonly believed, we hobby genealogists are not interested solely in proving descent from somebody famous; we also take satisfaction in discovering a relative who is just the opposite. There are even some who will argue that having an ancestor who "ran moonshine" is almost as good as discovering a great uncle who was hung for stealing a horse. There is even a degree of perverse satisfaction in proving that long-time family lore is incorrect. Naturally, I hoped this would not happen here.

Thus, in July of 1990, Ruth and I decided to drive from our home in Wisconsin to Western Pennsylvania, Northern Connecticut and four communities in Massachusetts. Our mission was to settle once and for all the family lore about the Standish connection. We planned to locate and visit the various places my ancestors had lived once they left Plymouth Colony. Additionally, along the way we would try to find each person's "vital records," especially the dates and places of their birth, marriage and death. (*)

In the one room school that I attended for eight years, American history was one of our most important subjects. At the time, I had not yet heard about the possible Myles Standish connection, but even so, the Pilgrim saga was extremely interesting to me. What I did not realize then was that our textbooks told a sanitized, romanticized version of Pilgrim events. Therefore, several chapters in this book are devoted to a much more factual description of the Colonists' trials and tribulations, including the effect of a plague they brought with them aboard the Mayflower. Half of them did not survive the first winter from the effects of the "General Sickness," exposure to the New England cold and lack of food.

Chapter One

FINDING CAPTAIN MYLES STANDISH

Forward

(*) Author's note: A parenthetical point should be made here for readers who might like to create a family genealogy of their own but assume it is no longer possible because the grandparent that "knew everything" has passed on. Although helpful, it is not necessary to have first-person recollections in order to build a family history. Anyone can obtain copies of relatives "vital records" from the deceased's local County Clerk or the Register of Deeds office, usually for about fifteen dollars and many of these same records can now be accessed online at the various county Web sites.

Richard Hafeman Haviland
N8337 North Shore Lane
Menasha, Wisconsin 54952

(920) 734-9930

Copyright 2009, all rights reserved
Published by BookSurge, a division of Amazon.com

Readers may also want to obtain my 2006 publication, "Splendid Gallantry," the untold story of the Union Army's XI Corps German-American Volunteers who fought and died at Chancellorsville, Gettysburg, and Sherman's March. This book is available from the author or online from Amazon.

Chapter Two

FINDING CAPTAIN MYLES STANDISH

SPICES, FURS, ADVENTURE COMPANIES

Captain John Smith (1580-1631)

When Henry VIII occupied the English throne for thirty-eight hectic years, he focused mainly on internal, marital and secular matters. It was not until his daughter Elizabeth became Queen in 1558 that the English resumed world exploration and colonizing. For various catastrophic reasons, some natural and some caused by poor planning, no Elizabethan colony lasted very long. Elizabeth's favored champion, Sir Walter Raleigh, led an ill-fated colonizing expedition to Roanoke, Virginia that lasted a mere two years.

In spite of this, glowing descriptions of profitable trading opportunities in the New World began to excite wealthy Englishmen who pooled their funds to build, buy or rent merchant ships which they sent off to the New World to trade for furs. In the spirit of the day, they were called "Adventure Companies." Adventuring was a chancy business. Merchant vessels were often lost to storms or pirates but, if they made it back home, it could be extremely profitable for the investors. It was soon obvious that, as with any other mercantile activity, friendly relations with the local Indians greatly improved the trader's chance of success. The key to this was obvious; colonists-traders with good public relation skills were needed to live among the Indians on a permanent basis.

Prior to any such trading adventure, it was necessary for the investors to obtain a "charter" from the King granting them exclusive trading rights for the lands which they wanted to exploit. The King expected a substantial share of the profits; royal treasuries required constant replenishment in order to finance armies, fight wars and maintain control of the populace. And, since pirates were a constant threat, the royal navy would be available to protect the royal investment.

Chapter Two

FINDING CAPTAIN MYLES STANDISH

SPICES, FURS, ADVENTURE COMPANIES

As European populations expanded, the need for new food sources also increased. Commercial fishermen from England and France began regular excursions to the Grand Banks off Newfoundland where the cod were so plentiful that fisherman claimed they could practically walk on waves of fish. Then, as now, fishermen tend to exaggerate.

Before the availability of refrigeration, preservation of the catch was a major problem. Fish caught at the Grand Banks had to be taken to nearby Newfoundland where they were placed upon racks and dried on shore after which they were packed in salt to be transported to England. Due to its strategic importance, Elizabeth decided to take possession of Newfoundland, thus creating her first colony. However, it turned into a costly undertaking when the very first English flotilla ran into a fierce storm that sank several ships and drowned the expedition's captain along with more than a hundred of his men.

The Queen's next colonization attempt was even more disastrous than the first. The Indians wiped out a small group of colonists left at Roanoke the first year. In the spring, when resupply ships arrived, the entire colony had vanished. Fifteen well-armed men were left on the island to hold it until resupply ships could return. Some months later when reinforcements arrived, the entire outpost had again been slaughtered. Several other English attempts to establish settlements in the New World also ended in complete failure. When Elizabeth died in 1603 and James I assumed the throne, a modification of the English colonization program was long overdue.

Merchant companies began sending ships to trade with Indians along the New England coast. Beaver hats had become extremely popular in Europe and trading for these valuable furs now took place from vessels that served as floating trading posts. Although this was a relatively low-risk way to do business, it was also very expensive. Without an on-shore resupply base, the vessels could not stay long before it was necessary to head back to England, full holds or empty.

Thirteen years prior to the sailing of the Mayflower, King James decided to try again to establish a colony, this one to be named Jamestown. Although the Indians were not responsible for destroying his colony, they did not need to bother; they very nearly starved on their own. It would, almost certainly, have perished but for the leadership of Captain John Smith--or so he would later claim.

Captain John Smith was a heroic, larger-than-life figure with an ego to match. A controversial leader, he was forever quarreling with his peers and frequently involved in power struggles. He became a much-in-demand speaker who, in 1610, had published "A Description of New England."
His book contained remarkably accurate maps of the New England coastline. Smith named one of the New England coastal harbors after the English port city of Plymouth.

Chapter Two

FINDING CAPTAIN MYLES STANDISH

SPICES, FURS, ADVENTURE COMPANIES

During his Jamestown venture, Smith often led wide-ranging expeditions deep into Indian Territory. During one such mission, hostile Indians captured him along with some of his men, all of whom were killed except Smith who managed to escape, later claiming he had been spared by the timely intervention of Pocahontas, daughter of the capturing Indian chief, Powhatan.

When Smith, the sole survivor, returned to the colony, he was arrested and tried for deserting the men under his command. His death sentence was about to be carried out when the arrival of another English ship brought a number of additional colonists who reversed the death sentence and he was set free. Taking no chances, Smith took the next ship back to England.

With the unabashed guile of an unprincipled real estate developer, Smith's book described in glowing prose the easy living and joys of carefree colony life in New England, neglecting entirely to mention that they had virtually starved.

Smith's shameless exaggerations were probably the chief reason why, from among a number of other possibilities, the Mayflower Pilgrims would eventually choose to go to Virginia. When they mistakenly landed much further north at Plymouth Harbor, they were totally unprepared for survival in the wild frontier, there or anywhere else. They arrived in the New World naively expecting to find a veritable Garden of Eden populated with welcoming tribesmen eager to trade with them. It did not happen.

Chapter Three

FINDING CAPTAIN MYLES STANDISH

ONE MAN ARMY

This sketch of Captain Myles Standish was not done from life and may or may not resemble him. Frankly, I think it portrays him as a bit of a fop and a trifle on the dainty side, something by all accounts he surely was not. In truth, Myles Standish was not an imposing figure. Short, sturdy and rather plump, he definitely did not cut a very heroic figure and certainly was not a very romantic one—as the fair Priscilla is supposed to have decided for herself.

Posthumous measurements of Standish's skeleton--his eternal rest being disturbed no less than three times—show that he was quite short even in a time when the average height for men was five feet eight inches. Some of the Indians called him "Captain Shrimp" partly due to his diminutiveness but mostly because of his fiery coloring when he became angry, a frequent occurrence.

Although the Puritans were opposed to portraiture of any kind, considering it as unholy self-glorification, Standish was not of their faith and presumably had no such scruples. Knowing this, one cannot help but wish that, before he left Leiden, his path would have crossed with that of young Rembrandt van Rijn who, in 1620, was only age 14 but had already attracted much local attention for his marvelous character sketches of the people he saw on the streets of Leiden (Leyden). If only he had given us one of the young Lt. Standish!

Chapter Three

FINDING CAPTAIN MYLES STANDISH

ONE MAN ARMY

For most of us, the Pilgrim Fathers have been fixed in our mind by children's coloring books. Smiling, smooth-shaven men in long black coats, knickers, white stockings and funny looking hats with broad buckles. Ladies are in full black skirts, starched white aprons and black bonnets. The well-fed children are dressed much the same, only in smaller sizes. The men folk tote smoothbore muskets in one hand, fat turkeys in the other. Nearby, clusters of contented Indians sit cross-legged, puffing pipes, patiently waiting to be served from heavily laden tables by the Pilgrim women.

Never illustrated is any hint of the dying and suffering they went through during their terrible first New England winter. Although Plimouth Colony (as it was spelled then) was the first continuously successful settlement in North America, the Mayflower was far from being the first ship to land in the New World. For one hundred and twenty years after Columbus, there were many, many ocean crossings by European fishermen, fur traders and explorers. And, several earlier English colonies had ended in utter disaster.

What made Plimouth succeed where the others failed so miserably? It certainly was not because they came better equipped, better supported or better trained to cope with all the trials they would face in the New World. Not all, but most historians agree that the success of Plymouth Colony was due mainly to one person—Captain Myles Standish. Historian Francis Dillon puts it this way:

> There was a one-man army aboard in the person of Captain Myles Standish . . . he was short, had reddish hair and a ruddy complexion, and he was an experienced soldier and a leader of men. (4)

Roland Usher, another Colony historian, agrees:

> He was admirably well placed in the colony, and the more one studies Pilgrim annals the larger he bulks, the greater his ability seems and the more important his services. His high personal courage, his resource-fullness, his great physical endurance, his fiery temper, all made him the leader needed to compliment the more peaceful and contemplative (Colony Governor) Bradford. (6) The Mayflower had thirty-four adult Puritans aboard, (they never referred to themselves as Pilgrims) and, although many of them were literate, few of them kept a journal or diary. The essential basis of Puritanism was that no one person stands above any other before the deity; all men were equal. The womenfolk, of course, were excepted. (6)

Chapter Three

FINDING CAPTAIN MYLES STANDISH

ONE MAN ARMY

Author-Historian Frances Dillon continues:

> The ordinary English left few records of the kind of people they were; they were frankly not interested in each other, there are no biographies whatsoever. What we know of them has to be gleaned from a few diaries and letters." (4)

Personal adornment was strictly discouraged, if not forbidden. Because Puritan clothing was so plain and utilitarian and since everyone dressed pretty much the same, they saw no reason to describe one another while later writing of colony activities. This is why there are so few clues, other than his size and coloring, concerning the appearance of the famous military leader of Plymouth Colony.

Colony Governor William Bradford later authored "The History of Plimouth Plantation," which provides us with the most detailed record of life in the early colony. Note: Where quotation marks are used without attribution, the reader should assume it is from Bradford.

Strangely, Bradford does not mention Standish until the Mayflower is safely anchored at Cape Cod. This is puzzling in that Standish would almost certainly have been involved in shipboard activities and decisions well before this; after all, he had been recruited to provide for the safety of the colony. As one of only thirty-four adult males on board the Mayflower, he must have been involved in dealing with the frequent crises arising during the crossing.

Was Standish, as some have suggested, merely a hired mercenary? Historian G.V.C. Young says definitely not:

> "It also seems clear that Myles Standish went to New England in a more important capacity than that of a hired employee. In this connection, it is material to note that Nathaniel Morton placed him as No. 6 in the hierarchy of the emigrants who sailed in the Mayflower...he is not included among the hired men." (10)

The following remarks were delivered at the 1870 dedication of the Standish monument some 150 years after his death. The orator obviously took Longfellow's "the Courtship of Myles Standish" at face value when he said, "No name in American history stands for greater courage and fearlessness, for greater boldness and more intrepid daring than the name of the man who had not the courage to speak for himself and ask the woman of his choice to be his wife."

Chapter Three

FINDING CAPTAIN MYLES STANDISH

ONE MAN ARMY

It was easier for Myles Standish to face a savage horde than it was for him to ask pretty and demure Priscilla Alden to be his wife. Faint heart has never yet won a fair lady, and one can imagine the chagrin of the unlucky wooer when he saw the fair Priscilla led to the altar by John Alden who evidently lost no time "speaking for himself." (1)

In his "History of Plimouth Colony," Bradford is extremely generous with his comments about the role Standish played in the survival of the Colony and makes clear that he is much appreciated by the rest of his Puritan employers as well. Such regard for a non-church member is quite unusual, the Puritans being famously intolerant of "strangers." Another notable exception was John Alden.

When his wife, Rose, perished from the plague the first winter at Plimouth, Myles sent back to England for what is generally assumed to be her younger sister Barbara, asking her to join him at the Colony as his wife. More than a century after the supposed event, Longfellow authored his famous poem, "The Courtship of Myles Standish," in which he portrays the Captain as being too timid to speak of his love directly to young Priscilla Mullen. He dispatched his friend, John Alden, to act as his emissary. "Why don't you speak for yourself, John," she is supposed to have said.

Longfellow claimed that this courtship tale had been handed down as part of his family lore, he being an Alden descendant. This could be true of course, but it seems unlikely that this event actually occurred, there being no other mention of it by anyone else at the time. Also, Longfellow portrays Standish as being very angry at John's perfidy but this too, fails to jibe with the fact that the Standishes and Aldens were lifelong friends and John and Priscilla's daughter eventually married Alexander, Myles and Barbara's oldest son.

Chapter Four

FINDING CAPTAIN MYLES STANDISH

Monstrous and Apparaunt Innovations

Early English monastery cathedral

How did it happen that members of a small, secret, forbidden congregation from the little community of Scrooby in Nottinghamshire abandoned their homes and property to go—first, across the English Channel to Holland and then over the Atlantic Ocean to the little-explored New World? To understand this, it is necessary to know more about the times in which the Puritan belief system gradually took root in strictest secret all over England.

Nearly one-third of all the arable land in England was owned by religious monasteries that the church leased to their parishioners at rates that kept them in perpetual serfdom. Even those religious orders supposedly committed to poverty and the simple life had become very wealthy, very powerful and very corrupt. The ordinary English farmer had few rights and little or no opportunity to improve his lot from one generation to another. The common folk were desperate for change in their way of life and the religion that kept them in never ending poverty and serfdom.

Chapter Four

FINDING CAPTAIN MYLES STANDISH

Monstrous and Apparaunt Innovations

In 1517, Pope Clement ordered his bishops to sell indulgences to parishioners that would be valid for eight years in advance—the more money paid—the more future sins to be forgiven. The bishops were instructed to keep half for local use, but send the balance to Rome to help pay for the construction of the Church of St. Peter, a monumental building project that was also monumentally expensive.

Martin Luther, a prior of eleven German Catholic friaries and a university professor already dissatisfied with what he considered to be the Church's excessive mercenary practices, decided to defy Roman authority. He nailed ninety-five objections to a local parish door. In doing so, he set in motion a chain of events far beyond anything he ever anticipated; the Christian world would never be the same.

Even before this, the Catholic Church had alienated many of its faithful. Luther touched a sensitive chord and his ideas quickly gained widespread support, thanks in part to Johannes Gutenberg's printing press, invented seventy years earlier and now in widespread use. It made possible wholesale circulation of Luther's Reformation concepts throughout all of Europe. He must have been very surprised when the English King, Henry VIII, publicly endorsed his views, even though he was motivated by other, less noble, personal reasons.

For some time, randy Henry had been attempting to persuade the Pope to annul his marriage to his first wife who was unable to bear him a male heir. He wanted dispensation to divorce her and marry his court favorite, but the Pope would have none of it.

Taking advantage of the convenient rising tide of anti-Catholic sentiment among his subjects, Henry forced the Act of Reformation through Parliament. These radical laws not only banned the Catholic Church and appropriated its vast wealth and property for the crown, it created an entirely new church with Henry himself the supreme ruler.

In remarkably short order, almost all Catholic monasteries were closed or destroyed. Ownership of church property passed to the Crown. A priest or bishop failing to convert to the new Church of England was banished on pain of death. The Act of Supremacy required all citizens to publicly swear allegiance to the King as head of church and state. Anyone who refused could be put to death.

All over England, citizens and families were sundered into either Protestant converts or secret Catholic loyalists. To encourage his subjects to back him against the banned Roman Church, Henry took a gamble and ordered the Holy Bible printed in English instead of Latin. This was an enormous change. Now for the first time the faithful did not need priests to instruct them in God's word; each man could read and interpret it for himself.

Chapter Four

FINDING CAPTAIN MYLES STANDISH

Monstrous and Apparaunt Innovations

The English Bible was welcomed by the masses, but there were unintended consequences; his subjects began questioning not only the Pope's right to dictate religious matters but the validity of Henry's church as well. The Church of England rites were much the same as the Catholic's with the same gaggle of priests, bishops and cardinals. Even worse, they still were extracting money from the faithful to maintain the opulent lifestyle of the church hierarchy.

All over England, doubters and dissenters began meeting in secret; to do otherwise was to invite the wrath of both Church and Crown, who considered any challenges to their authority to be treasonous and, therefore, punishable by death. Even so, increasingly stronger objections were being raised throughout the domain. Here and there, religious sects began to form, meeting in deepest secrecy and at great personal peril.

Henry VIII occupied the English throne for thirty-eight years, his focus mainly on internal, marital and secular matters. After Henry's death in 1547, his sickly young son, Edward, reigned only briefly before he also died, after which his older sister, Mary, next in line, became queen. She had remained a staunch Catholic and had never converted to her father's church. Upon assuming the throne, Mary promptly outlawed the Church of England, ordering her subjects to revert to Catholicism or face the prospect of being burned at the stake.

Mary also obligated the very same bishops that Henry had deposed to help root out all her subjects who had renounced the Church of Rome, a chore they fell to with relish and the torture and burnings continued. English heresy trials began in 1555. Some sixty prominent churchmen were burned alive for failing to swear obedience to the Queen. As they became ever more skilled in the art of extracting "confessions," the inquisitor's net soon widened to the common folk as well as to the "turncoat" clergy.

In 1556, church records state "there were burned 80 persons, whereof many were maidens." The following year the same record adds: "In this year were burnt about London more than 64, whereof 20 were women." These increased immolations created numbers of martyrs, causing many additional secret anti-Catholic congregations to organize, all of them committed to separation from the Church of Rome. They called themselves "Separatists".

The common folk—those who could read—studied the new Bible carefully and could find no mention of Pope, Bishop or even priests. They reasoned that, since it was not specified in the Bible, the entire hierarchical church structure was nothing more than an unholy invention of mortal men like themselves. These secret sects, seldom numbering more than two hundred, gradually coalesced around a philosophy that held that any group could separate from the Church and organize themselves as a congregation with the right to choose their own teachers and elders.

Chapter Four

FINDING CAPTAIN MYLES STANDISH

Monstrous and Apparaunt Innovations

Further, every man had a right to vote in actions of the congregation, a radical concept that was anathema to both Church and Crown. This religious philosophy gradually evolved into an ever-stricter code of personal conduct that practically eliminated any pleasurable act. They called themselves the "Church of Purity," eventually shortening it to just "Puritans."

Much despised by her subjects, Mary died childless in 1557, with the burnings continuing almost to the hour of her death. Her much younger half-sister Elizabeth ascended to the throne and immediately ordered the inquisitions and burnings to cease.

Elizabeth promptly reinstated the church of her father and once again, English citizens were forced to switch faiths. Although more tolerant of religious dissent than her sister, Elizabeth disapproved of any doctrine that questioned higher authority, hers or that of the church. She issued a proclamation against "diffamatorie and fantasticall" writings, stating emphatically that such ideas were "monstrous and apparaunt innovations."

But the concept of religious freedom had gained too much of a foothold to be put down by royal wrath or even royal decree. It continued to expand even after authors of several offensive religious writings were hanged for treason, along with the press owners that printed them. Hundreds more citizens were jailed for publicly expressing contrary religious beliefs. In 1593, Elizabeth made attendance in the Church of England mandatory. "Any persons who absent themselves from the orthodox service for more than a month, or who attempts in any way to persuade others to do so, or who attends any unlawful assemblies, conventicles, or meetings under colour or pretense of and Exercise of Religion will be imprisoned without bail."

Obviously, embracing a new or unorthodox religion was not something to be done lightly. If found guilty, culprits had six months in prison to repent after which they were banished forever; if they returned to England, they were arrested and put to death. Even so, families all over England continued converting to various other new splinter faiths.

About 1606, a group of approximately fifty persons began meeting secretly in the chapel of an unused royal hunting preserve located at Scrooby in northern England. They were mostly local farmers of limited education but three of them were university graduates, tutored mainly in Greek and Latin theology.

One such student was William Brewster, son of the Scrooby postmaster. Another was William Bradford, then about eighteen. (He would eventually become Governor of Plymouth Colony and its principal historian). A third was John Robinson, a Cambridge student of about thirty who would become principal theologian and teacher of the Scrooby congregation.

Chapter Four

FINDING CAPTAIN MYLES STANDISH

Monstrous and Apparaunt Innovations

These three men provided the principal impetus that eventually caused the Scrooby worshippers to abandon farms and homes to relocate across the Channel in Holland. By this time, many of the new secret religious sects had become bitter enemies, as intolerant of contrary viewpoints as were the Catholics or the Church of England. At the urging of Robinson, Brewster and Bradford, the Scrooby brethren decided to form a new Puritan congregation that, predictably, was soon regarded with extreme derision and suspicion by their neighbors.

Contrary to what is now commonly believed, it was not just persecution by the Crown or Church that forced the Scrooby Puritans to abandon their homeland. Colony historian, William Bradford, later wrote that he could never forget or forgive the constant jeering and derision of neighbors whose hostility was the main reason they decided to leave England. Some months earlier, another similar group had gone to Holland and sent word back that they liked it there very much. Once the Scrooby Congregation decided to go, it did not take them long to prepare. Since they, as tenants, owned no property and had few worldly goods, pulling up stakes was relatively easy to do.

Carrying their meager possessions on their backs, they walked to a small nearby port where they had arranged for a suitable vessel to take them across the channel to Holland. However, when they got there and prepared to board, a law forbidding removal from the country of any gold and silver caused the arrest of several members. After being held for a nearly a month, they were finally released and sent back to Scrooby where they faced increased hostility from their former neighbors.

As soon as they were able, the congregation chartered another ship. This time they chose a more secluded boarding site and kept their departure date a solemn secret. Just as they were about to board, misfortune struck again when the receding tide caused the vessel to be stuck fast on a hidden sand bar. While they were waiting for the rising tide to free the craft, angry locals approached the stranded ship and fearing violence, the nervous master sailed off with some of the Puritans aboard, separating families and leaving others to face the mob. The local constabulary saved them from mayhem. With no real desire to keep them in jail, authorities soon permitted them to "escape" and go aboard the ship still standing offshore.

As is often the case with the English Channel, it was a very rough crossing. A storm with mighty waves frightened even the experienced crew. Everyone feared sinking until the Puritans "fell upon their knees and prayed for deliverance." Bradford credits these prayers for saving the ship. They finally arrived safely in Amsterdam in the autumn of 1608.

Chapter Five

FINDING CAPTAIN MYLES STANDISH

EXCESSIVE JOYILITY

Spanish King Phillip was determined to force his Catholic faith upon his Dutch neighbors and was well known for slaughtering Protestants unlucky enough to fall under his control. Phillip was at least partly responsible for the Scrooby congregation's decision to seek sanctuary elsewhere. The Dutch people loved a good time and it was not long before the strait-laced Puritans became concerned with what they considered excessive "joyility."

The merry Dutchmen especially loved singing and dancing, both activities considered by the Puritans to be especially sinful. The Leydener lifestyle quickly became anathema to them and, even more alarming, Puritan children were happily adapting to their new surroundings. The idea of their children marrying into such a decadent society was more than the elders could tolerate.

Although the Puritan immigrants could worship as they wished, life was hard. With few exceptions, they were limited to lower-paying, menial employment. The better paying craftsmen jobs required guild membership and in order to join a guild, one first had to become a Dutch citizen.

Chapter Five

FINDING CAPTAIN MYLES STANDISH

EXCESSIVE JOYILITY

Additionally, the temporary peace with Spain was about to end and renewal of a winner-take-all religious war with such a fanatic enemy was an especially daunting prospect. It was well known that King Phillip demanded his subjects convert to the Catholic faith or face the prospect of being burned alive at the stake.

> They lived here as men in exile, and in a poor condition; and as great miseries might Befall them in this place for the twelve years of truce (with Spain) were now nearly ended; and there was nothing but beating of drums and preparing for war, the events of which are always uncertain. (2)

They decided they must leave Holland, but how and where could they go?

First, they had to secure financial backing. For twelve years they had worked hard, paid their bills, and developed good credit but they were still unable to finance a major relocation to another continent or even another country. To equip, transport, protect and feed themselves they had to find a willing sponsor to underwrite their relocation expenses.

For some time, glowing descriptions by John Smith and others describing the magnificent trading opportunities in the New World had been exciting wealthy Englishmen. Many of them formed corporations with pooled funds to build, buy or rent merchant ships which they sent off to the New World to trade for spices, furs and other profitable goods. In the spirit of the day, they were called "Adventure Companies." In return for a generous share of the profits, the King would grant them large parcels of land, mostly along the North American Atlantic coast and use the Royal Navy to provide their trading vessels with protection from piracy.

This mutually profitable arrangement was largely responsible for expanding the English presence throughout the world. Still, adventuring was a chancy business. Merchant vessels were often lost to storms or pirates but if they made it back home, it could be extremely profitable for the investors and colonists. It was soon realized that, as with any other mercantile activity, friendly relations with the locals greatly improved the odds of success. The key to this success was obvious; hard-working colonists were needed with good public relation skills. The Puritans were aware that several of these corporations had already attempted to establish trading outposts in New England and that all of them had ended in utter disaster.

Chapter Five

FINDING CAPTAIN MYLES STANDISH

EXCESSIVE JOYILITY

The Virginia Company had quite recently received a special charter from King James granting exclusive trading rights along the Virginia coast. In order to exploit their franchise properly, the Virginia Adventurers needed agents willing to live where the action was and establish friendly relations with the Indians, whose good will was vital if they were to obtain the valuable furs so prized in Europe. The Puritans were confident that with God's help they could succeed where others had failed.

It is unclear whether the Scrooby congregation contacted the Virginia Adventure Company or it was the other way around. At any rate, after the customary lengthy discussions that always preceded any congregational action, several elders were delegated to go to England to negotiate sponsorship by the Virginia Company. In the spring of 1620, the Puritan emissaries carried back to Holland a sponsorship offer from Virginia Company agent, John Weston.

A seven-year communal partnership would be created in which all goods, food, equipment and homes would belong to the Company to be held as common stock. The colonists would endeavor to add to the value of the common stock while the investors would agree to supply whatever else they needed to accomplish the common goal.

The agreement was simple and straightforward. Trading and fishing activities would accrue profits in England for the partnership's benefit. The colonists agreed to work four days per week for the good of the partnership and two days for themselves, improving the colony. After seven years, all debts would be paid and the colony and its improved lands would belong to the colonists. They and the venture capitalists would profit handsomely.

It seemed like a perfect marriage. The Puritans needed sponsorship and the Virginia Company seemed to be the answer to their prayers; a company with deep pockets was just what they needed.

The Virginia Company, too, believed they had paired up with the ideal partners; pious, hard working, dependable farmers and skilled craftsmen who would honor their commitments. It did not take long for an agreement to be drawn up for the elders to take back to Leyden for ratification.

Chapter Five

FINDING CAPTAIN MYLES STANDISH

EXCESSIVE JOYILITY

ARTICLES OF AGREEMENT

1. The Adventurers and Planters do agree that every person that goeth, age 16 years and upward be rated at 10 Pounds and that this be counted as a single share.
2. Each settler furnishing himself out with 10 Pounds or other provisions shall be accounted to have 20 Pounds so in the division of assets (at the conclusion of the contract) shall have double share.
3. The partnership between the adventurers and the settlers shall last at least seven years, during which time all profits shall remain in the common stock.
4. After landing, some will be employed in fishing at sea and the rest building houses and farming the land.
5. After seven years, capital and profits including houses, lands, goods and chattels to be divided equally between adventurers and Settlers, after which each side shall be clear of each other.
6. Any latecomer or investor shall receive his proportionate share.
7. Wives, children or servants over 16 have a single share, a double share if "furnished out." Children between 10 and 16 a half share.
8. Children now fewer than ten no share other than 50 acres of unaltered (land).
9. Executors (survivors) to have the proportionate share of any land.
10. All settlers to have food and clothing out of the common stock.

Even before the negotiators returned to Leyden, the congregation began discussing how they wanted to live and where that should be. They poured over primitive travel brochures and travel guides of the day. Among the ones they considered most interesting were Sir Walter Raleigh's recently published "Discoverie of the Large Rich and Beautiful Empire of Guiana," Whitaker's, "Good News from Virginia" and Captain John Smith's, "A Description of New England."

Chapter Five

FINDING CAPTAIN MYLES STANDISH

EXCESSIVE JOYILITY

Raleigh's glowing description of Guiana caused many to argue in its favor:

> "... a rich, fruitful and blessed land with a perpetual spring, where nature brought forth all things in abundance without any great labor or art of man. So as it must needs make the inhabitants rich, seeing less provision of clothing and other things would serve them in colder and less fruitful countries must be had." (2)

To some of the would-be colonists, Guiana sounded like paradise. Others argued it was too good to be true. After more discussion, they agreed upon Virginia. Actually, they did not have any choice; the Virginia Company was the only one willing to sponsor them and their charter from the King specified Virginia.

> When the negotiators returned to Leyden, they were surprised to find that not all of the members were pleased with what they had done. But as in all business, the acting part is the most difficult, especially where the work of many agents must concur; for some of those that should have gone who were in England fell off and would not go, merchants and friends that had offered to adventure money withdrew, and pretended many excuses. Some disliking they would not go to Guiana, others again would adventure nothing except they went to Virginia. Some again—and those that were most relied on—fell into utter dislike with Virginia and would do nothing if they went thither. (9)

The core of Puritan belief was a simple, easily understood principle that permitted no religious superior to stand between a man and his God. However, they had no problem acknowledging the existence of social inferiors, as one of them later wrote:

Chapter Five

FINDING CAPTAIN MYLES STANDISH

EXCESSIVE JOYILITY

> They believed that God had ordained that in all times some must be rich, some poor, some high and eminent in power and authority; others mean and in subjugation. (4)

Obviously, the Puritans were not willing to apply the concept of equality to everyone; women were treated respectfully but seldom included in "serious" discussions—that was men's work. All who could afford to do so took servants with them to New England, many of them homeless orphans. And once they got there, it is not difficult to guess whom they planned to subjugate.

From a painting by artist George Catlin

Chapter Six

FINDING CAPTAIN MYLES STANDISH

Good-natured and Immensely Fat

Although I did not learn of a possible connection with Captain Myles Standish until I stayed with Grandmother Tory during my freshman year in high school, my interest in family history matters began long before that. One of the advantages of being the eldest of nine children was that before too many siblings came along, I was able to listen to adult table conversation, usually about neighbors, but the subject often turned to more interesting gossip about relatives. Fascinating stuff indeed. I especially enjoyed helping my favorite Aunt Blanche place flowers on family graves for Decoration Day, as it was then called. We usually did a half-dozen different cemeteries with our final visit always at the grave of Calvin Young, her grandfather and my great-grandfather, at the flag-lined Civil War Veterans Circle at the city's Evergreen Cemetery. Calvin was about age sixty-four when Blanche, his youngest granddaughter, was born. He and his wife Matilda lived with Tory and her children for the next eleven years until he died. Actually, it was the other way around since Andrew Haviland had left his wife and five young children to return to his former home in Michigan.

As far as his children were concerned, Andrew Jackson Haviland seems to have been more shadow than substance. To be fair he may have tried to keep in touch with his children, but if he did, Tory was not about to permit it. When he left them, around 1915, Josephine was about age 19, Hazel, 17, Lila, 15, George, 13, and Blanche, 11. As adults, none of them had much to say about their father, at least in my presence. When he died in 1943, the girls went to his Saginaw funeral (Hazel had died in childbirth in 1924), but George refused to go. "He was nothing to me," I heard him say at the time.

Although normally good-natured and fun to be with, the mere mention of Andrew's name was enough to set Tory off on a volcanic diatribe that was not pretty to see. After trying several times to find out something about my grandfather with the same result, I never brought it up again. However, it did give me a better understanding of why Andrew may have left her in the first place.

I asked Blanche to tell me what great-grandfather Calvin was like. She recalled how they often walked slowly to the back pasture where they sat under an old fruit tree. If asked about his war service he would only say, "It was rough, very rough." He was good-natured and "immensely fat," so that two extra men were required to carry his funerary casket. To this day, his genes are still evident in many of his great-grandchildren, I among them.

Chapter Six

FINDING CAPTAIN MYLES STANDISH

Good-natured and Immensely Fat

Although this bit of information about Calvin was interesting, I wanted to know more and wrote to the Veteran's Administration in Washington to request copies of Cal's military records. Of course, there were several documents for me to fill out to get them but eventually I received the information for which I was looking.

Additional reading showed that after the 1863 Battle of Chickamauga, there were so many Union casualties—more than 17,000 killed, wounded or captured—that fresh recruits had to be found or the war could easily be lost. Shortly before Christmas that year, a recruiting rally was held in the little village of Wattsburg, Pennsylvania, just east of the Ohio border. Calvin, then age 23, enlisted in the 125th Ohio Volunteers, known as "Updike's Tigers," after their esteemed Colonel, Emerson Updike.

From my growing library of Civil War books, I learned that the 125th Ohio was one of General William Tecumseh Sherman's attached regiments during his famous march to Atlanta. Before getting there, Cal's regiment participated in a series of bloody battles all across upper Georgia: Rocky Face Ridge; Resaca; New Hope Church; Dallas; Kennesaw Mountain; Big Shanty and Peach Tree Creek, finally arriving at Sherman's main objective, the City of Atlanta.

Some years later, while I was doing research for my 215-page book about the 26th Wisconsin Volunteers ("Splendid Gallantry"), I realized that the 26th Wisconsin, had also been part of General Sherman's vast army during his famous march to Atlanta and that both regiments had fought in the same series of battles all the way to Atlanta. (*)

My interest in our family's Young-Standish ancestry, long dormant, was unexpectedly rekindled by a 1989 phone call from a gentleman who identified himself as Walter Young, of Elkhart, Indiana. He explained that he had been trying for years to locate kinfolk he knew lived somewhere in Wisconsin. We compared notes and, to our mutual delight, discovered that our respective great-grandfathers Calvin and Standish Young were brothers, making the two of us third cousins. Tory had been right about that much, at the very least.

As every genealogist will agree, one of the most rewarding aspects of family research is the discovery of a previously unknown relative who is able to provide just the information for which you had been long searching. Of course, it is even better when you can fill in gaps for them.

Chapter Six

FINDING CAPTAIN MYLES STANDISH

Good-natured and Immensely Fat

We invited Walter to come to Wisconsin for a get-acquainted visit and we found we genuinely liked each other, this being the reason Ruth and I made a detour to Elkhart on our research trip to the East Coast. We spent a half day and evening with Walter and Chris and found them to be extremely congenial hosts. At the time, Chris was a very busy real estate agent while Walter, a retired Air Force colonel who had flown B-52's, was now the personal pilot for the chairman of a national manufacturer of recreational vehicles headquartered at Elkhart.

According to Walter, our mutual great-great grandfather was Alonzo Young, a pioneer farmer in Amity Township, Erie County, Pennsylvania. He also said that Alonzo's mother was Amy Standish Young, who was living with him when she died. This was exactly the link between the Young and the Standish families that I had been hoping to verify. Although Walter had been aware of the family lore claiming a distant family connection to Myles Standish, he had not researched Amy's parentage and did not know of any documentation that would establish her lineage.

Alonzo Young, our mutual 3rd great grandfather, was born 1803 in Ashfield, Massachusetts and died in Erie County, Pennsylvania in 1879. His parents were John Young and Amy Standish. Walter was sure of their existence and their marriage, but did not know where or when it had taken place.

After his first wife, Seloma, died, Alonzo married Mary Ann Holcomb in 1836. Their children, all born in Amity Township, were: Elizabeth, b.1836; William, b. 1839; Calvin, b. 1840; Standish, b. 1841; Zephaniah, b. 1843; Rhoda, b. 1845; Amelia, b.1847; Emma, b.1849; and Alice, b.1851.

After Alonzo died in 1875, his son, Standish, worked the farm until he died in 1907, when it was willed to his son, Frank. When Frank passed away, his son, Nelson, Walter's father, ended the family tradition by selling the farm to a neighbor.

Thus it was, that in late June of 1990, Ruth and I left for points east, feeling almost adventurous. Our mission was to trace—in reverse—the westward migration of our Standish ancestors as each succeeding generation followed the frontier from Plymouth farther westward. Over several years, I had assembled from copies of birth, marriage and death certificates the location where these various ancestors had been born, married and buried.

Chapter Six

FINDING CAPTAIN MYLES STANDISH

Good-natured and Immensely Fat

Our first stop was at the Forest Lawn Cemetery in Saginaw, Michigan, where Grandfather Andrew Haviland is buried. This stop was in the nature of a "courtesy call;" my interest on the first stage of our trip was focused not on Andrew, but on his father, Calvin, the Civil War veteran. By this time, I had copies of his enlistment documents and knew that Calvin had volunteered for service at the little Village of Wattsburg, near where he lived at the time. I wanted to go there and Walter said he would be happy to come along and be our guide; things were off to a good start.

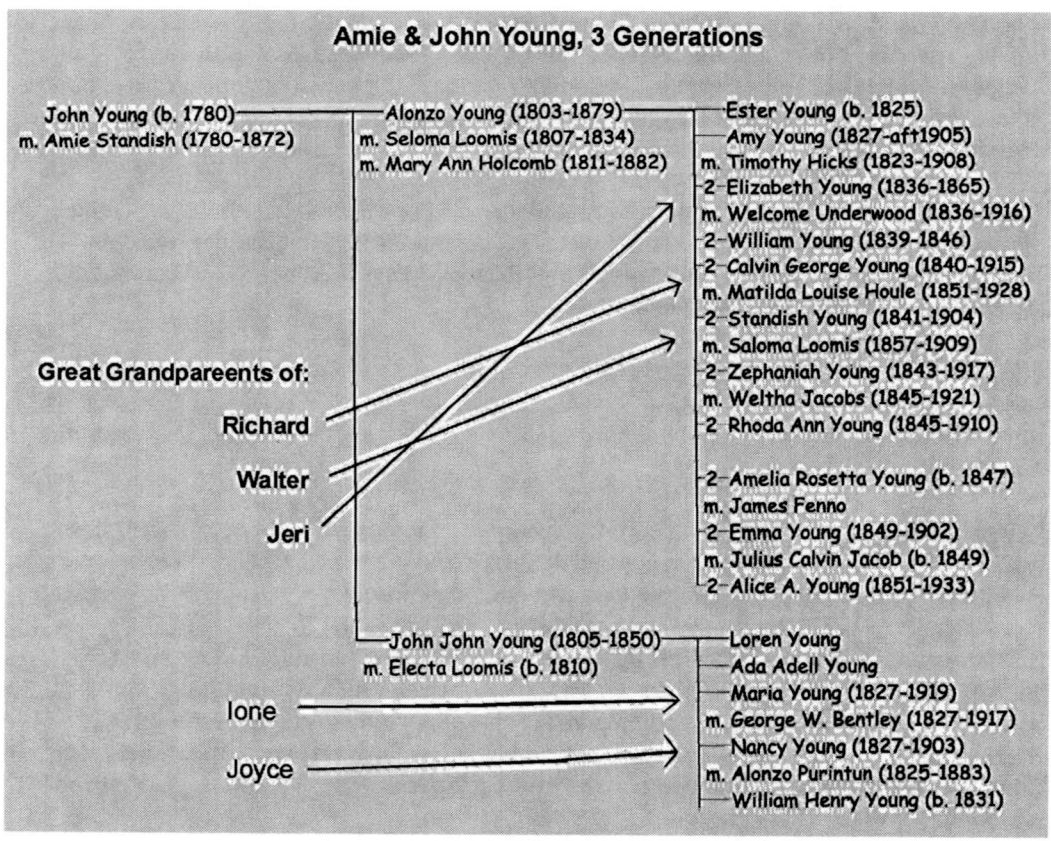

Chapter Six

FINDING CAPTAIN MYLES STANDISH

Good-natured and Immensely Fat

Presented all at once, the information in this chapter is probably confusing to anyone not previously involved in ancestry research. Hopefully, it will become clearer as the reader continues. The following chart may help; this simplified diagram also includes the names of other family researchers and how they connect to various family members.

In addition to Walter and me, they are: Jeri Pope Kemmer of Salmon, Idaho along with contributors Ione Cumberland and Ada Ball Cass, both now deceased.

Author's note:

A one-in-a-million coincidence came to light while I was researching Civil War military records for my earlier book, "Splendid Gallantry," published in 2006 by BookSurge, a division of Amazon.

The first book had nothing to do with Corporal Calvin Haviland—or so I thought—it was about the Twenty-Sixth Wisconsin Volunteers and the Civil War Service of Carl Hafemann, an entirely different great-grandfather, this one on my mother's side of the family.

Hafemann was struck by a Minie ball in the left leg just as the Twenty-Sixth Wisconsin moved up to relieve the beleaguered 125th Ohio at the Battle of Dallas, Georgia, just north of Atlanta.

Of course Carl and Calvin did not know each other and never met after the war, both men died well before their respective grandchildren—my parents—Ruby Hafeman and George Haviland married in 1931.

(*) "Splendid Gallantry", is available online from Amazon.com or directly from the Author for $27.50, postage prepaid.

Chapter Six

FINDING CAPTAIN MYLES STANDISH

Good-natured and Immensely Fat

This picture of Victoria and Andrew, probably a wedding photograph, which I have dated accordingly, is the only one of the two of them together that I have ever seen. I am no longer sure which of their daughters squirreled it away and gave it to me after Tory died but I am quite certain that she did not know of its existence. Much to my regret, I have never seen a photo of Calvin.

Victoria and Andrew Haviland

Chapter Seven

FINDING CAPTAIN MYLES STANDISH

As I Remember It

Walter and his sister Pat were quite small when their parents (Nelson and Dorcas) divorced. This was the reason why they spent so much time on the farm with their grandparents, Frank and Golda Young. When Walter learned that we were planning to visit the old Young homestead, he said he would pick up his sister Pat Baird, who lived nearby, and they would meet us there. We were, of course, extremely pleased to have them join us.

To help set the stage for our visit to the site of our great-great grandfather's farm, Walter gave us a copy of an essay written by Alonzo Young's granddaughter, Nora Fenno. "Our Family Record as I Remember It," is a charming, nostalgic essay, written seven years before she passed away in 1935.

__Our Family Record as I Remember It __

Nora Fenno Frederick   (1887-1935)

My grandfather & grandmother, Mary Ann cleared the land and built a three room log house where they lived for several years and all their children were born there. In those days, the houses were heated with stone fireplaces. The stone was taken from the land they were clearing. They did all their cooking by the fireplace. All the children who were born in the old log home were Elizabeth, William, Calvin, Standish, Zephaniah, Rhoda, Amelia (my mother), Emma and Alice. Alice was three years old when they built the new house, which had six rooms. Then they bought a cook stove and a heater for the kitchen and living room, but my Grand parents still clung to the fireplace and built one in one room, which they called their sitting room. It was built of birch with mantles at each end and burned four-foot logs. This room was the gathering place for all the family as well as their neighbors and friends. Grandfather made all the furniture. They raised everything they ate, also tobacco and herbs for medicine, such as Thyme, Wormwood, Mint, Pennyroyal, Sage and Summer Savory, Caraway, Dill, Horse Radish and always gathered herbs from the fields and woods.

Chapter Seven

FINDING CAPTAIN MYLES STANDISH

As I Remember It

As the boys grew larger of course, they helped to clear the land. They set out a nice orchard and grandfather brought Pear seed from his native state Mass. and planted it in the orchard. The Pear tree is now standing and bears the grandest fruit every year. The old orchard consisted of all kinds of apples, pears and several kinds of peaches, cherries, plums and grapes.

My grandfather dug a well by the side of the new house, built a smokehouse, corncrib, barns and other out buildings. This new house was a frame building; the logs were sawed on the first sawmill in that section of the country, and was once owned by Jonathan Hill. Soon after Grandfather bought this place, he gave a small lot on the corner for a schoolhouse. The neighbors all turned in and built a log schoolhouse, where all their children went to school. After the little Sawmill started, they built a new frame schoolhouse where the old log school building stood, it having burned in 1922.

My Grandfather (Alonzo) had the nicest maple grove and made lots of maple sugar and syrup and vinegar which they used, and they traded for white sugar, tea and coffee, salt, black pepper and spices that they couldn't raise. They always cured their own meat such as smoked hams and shoulders, canned sausage, pickled side meat, besides they always kept fresh pork and beef frozen all winter. They dried beef and corned beef, made their own mincemeat, raisins, jelly, vinegar besides all kinds of preserves and dried fruit.

They raised sheep and cattle, geese, turkeys and chickens so they had plenty of fresh meat and eggs in the summer. They raised flax for flax seed meal. They carded and spun their own linens and wool and wove their own cloth for clothes, table linens, blankets and counterpanes. Knit hose, mittens and gloves, lace caps, crocheted curtains, spreads, lace and they were happy.

Chapter Seven

FINDING CAPTAIN MYLES STANDISH

As I Remember It

The Eagle Hotel, Waterford, PA

It was quite late in the day when we reached the outskirts of the city of Erie in western Pennsylvania. We checked into a convenient motel and decided to use the remaining daylight to continue on to the little village of Wattsburg where, in 1863, Great grandfather Calvin volunteered for service in the Union Army. We intended to have our dinner at a Wattsburg restaurant but we traveled the length of the village main street before realizing that we had seen all there was to see and there was no eatery. With a population of just 350, the village is only slightly larger today than it was when Calvin enlisted there 130 years earlier.

We continued on to the nearby village of Waterford, a community numbering a bit over 3,000. It was most serendipitous as we found Waterford to be a charming and extremely interesting place, steeped in history. Mainly because of its ancient appearance, we decided to dine at the Eagle Hotel, a charming well preserved, two-story, stone structure with what was obviously still a popular dining room. The decor was perfect—straight out of the mid to late 1800's.

Chapter Seven

FINDING CAPTAIN MYLES STANDISH

As I Remember It

Our excellent dinner, enhanced by our customary pre-dinner cocktail, was made even more enjoyable by the thought that it was possible, even probable, that our ancestors, who lived no more than a dozen miles distant, may have dined there as well. We ordered a bottle of wine with dinner, admired the food, the service, the decor, and began to feel ourselves meld into a long ago time period. When we left the hotel, it was almost shocking to find our automobile sitting at the curb instead of a wagon and team of horses. It may have been that last glass of wine.

After breakfasting the next morning at the home of Pat Baird, the four of us drove on to the farm that Alonzo had carved out of the wilderness a century and a half earlier. Enroute, we enjoyed listening to Walter and Pat tell stories of the happy times they spent with grandparents Frank and Golda Young during their summer vacations.

The Amity township terrain was quite a bit hillier and surrounded by more woodlands than had been imagined. I had incorrectly assumed that, the area having been settled so long ago, the countryside would now be quite open and much more densely populated. Instead, it was reminiscent of today's Northern Wisconsin.

Thinking more on the subject, I could see why this was so; the first settlers wrested the land from thick forest at great cost and then, after decades of unimaginable labor, younger generations began looking for a better paying, easier life elsewhere. Gradually, the trees and the scrub bushes took back the land that was once theirs. Then, commuting hobby farmers salvaged what they could without expending too much effort.

The better surrounding farmland had been gradually acquired by farming entrepreneurs with the necessary capitol and machinery to do it right. Probably because eastern Pennsylvania is situated on the extreme eastern edge of the ancient Wisconsin Glacier, the soil left behind twelve thousand years ago is generally thin and stoney, mostly unsuitable for large-scale production farming. A few miles distant, the ice-melt lake bottoms are flatter and the loamy soil richer and more productive. A topographical map shows that a good portion of the less desirable farmland has been acquired by the state, probably for back taxes, and is now designated as public game lands. Ironically, the circle is now complete. Although no one now lives on the old Young property, it was not lying fallow; the land is being worked as part of a large neighboring farm operation.

Chapter Seven

FINDING CAPTAIN MYLES STANDISH

As I Remember It

The frame house so lovingly described by Nora Fenno as "new" burned down many years ago and the old barn and most of the out buildings are gone as well. Very little remains of what once was a busy, self-sufficient homestead excepting of course, the memories. While Pat had lived there during most of her childhood years, Walter was there just during summer vacations. We stood together near where the old house had been and Walter and Pat shared a few more recollections of gatherings of grandparents, uncles, aunts and cousins. Having grown up on a farm myself, their memories were often my memories as well.

It being quite unlikely that I would ever come this way again, I resolved that someday I would write about it, perhaps encouraging others who might want to see this site themselves. I took some photographs but have not used them here; without any buildings in the scene, it could have been anywhere.

After taking one last look around, we headed westerly down the old Wattsburg road a half mile or so to the site where the Young schoolhouse once stood. Not only Alonzo's children went there, but also his grandchildren and great grand children as well, all of them taught by the same teacher.

Our next stop was the Beaver Dam Cemetery, a dozen or so miles away, a tree shaded, well tended and very peaceful final resting place. Beaver Dam Creek, from which it takes its name, borders it on one side. Walter and Pat guided us past rows of ancient monuments, the chiseled lettering barely legible. We soon came to the graves of Alonzo and Mary Ann Young. Just beyond were headstones identifying the graves of Standish and Seloma as well as Frank and Golda. If there was a headstone for Amy Standish Young, I did not see it, possibly because the lettering had deteriorated beyond recognition.

We thanked Pat and Walter for their hospitality and said our goodbyes, promised to keep in touch and departed for our next destination, Mansfield, Connecticut, five hundred miles farther east.

Chapter Seven

FINDING CAPTAIN MYLES STANDISH

As I Remember It

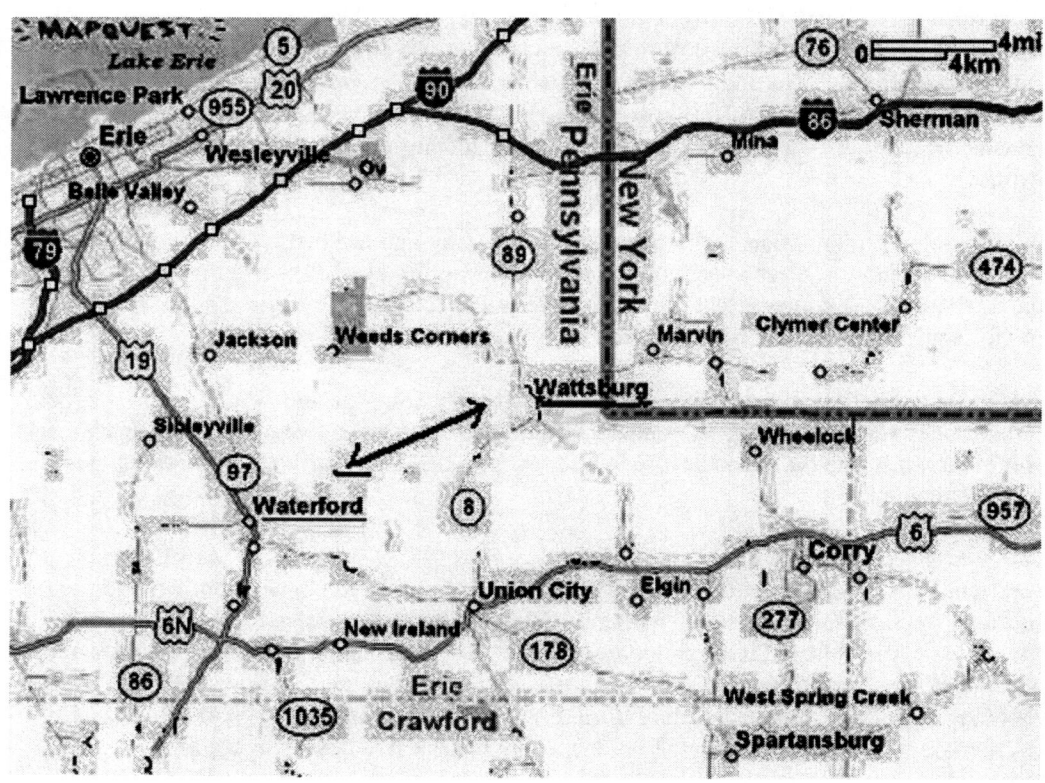

Erie, Wattsburg, Waterford vicinity

Chapter Eight

FINDING CAPTAIN MYLES STANDISH

LOATHE TO DEPART

Going aboard the Speedwell

Following months of earnest negotiations, the Scrooby Puritans and the Virginia Company finally came to terms. It was agreed that a trading post would be established from which they would obtain furs and other items from the Indians and that they would themselves commercially fish the Grand Banks. Additionally, the Puritans were to cut and export lumber, collect sassafras and ship other medicinal roots and herbs back to England.

Once the contract was finalized and letters of credit arranged, the Puritans hired agents in London and Dartmouth to assemble needed equipment and supplies. These men, known as chandlers, were critical to the success of the expedition—but as they would discover when it was too late—the colonists should have chosen more carefully and supervised more closely.

The lack of reliable information about Myles Standish's early years is frustrating to historians. Exactly when it was that Standish became associated with the Scrooby Puritans is unclear; but it was almost certainly well before this time that the Puritan elders recruited him to accompany them as their "military advisor." Before long, they would wish devoutly that their chandlers would have served them half so well.

Chapter Eight

FINDING CAPTAIN MYLES STANDISH

LOATHE TO DEPART

A prominent Isle of Man historian, G.V.C. Young, has distilled most of what little is known about Standish's early life. Young's definitive work (see bibliography) is the basis for much of what is presented here regarding Standish's pre-Mayflower history.

Young writes that Myles was about age seventeen when, in 1601, he left his father's estate at Ellanbane on the Isle of Man just off the western coast of England to begin a career in the British military. As was the custom, his father probably purchased for him a lieutenant's commission and, after brief military indoctrination, he was sent as part of a 3,000-man expedition to Holland where the Dutch had long been involved in a bitter war with Spanish King Phillip. Queen Elizabeth believed that the best way to keep the Spanish Catholics at bay was to fight them alongside the Dutch on Dutch territory.

The Spanish siege of Ostend lasted for three years and is one of the longest in history. It ended with a negotiated twelve-year truce (1609-1621). It has been said of it that, "the Spanish assailed the unassailable and the Dutch defended the indefensible."

This war would last for a total of eighty years and doubtless had much to do with the Puritans decision to leave Holland. It also may have influenced Standish's decision to leave the British army and seek employment elsewhere.

Author Young cites evidence that shows Standish was wounded at the Battle of Ostend where 140,000 men were killed and thousands more wounded. The extent of his battle injuries is not clear although they were obviously very serious. He was admitted to St. Catherine's Hospital in nearby Leyden on October 18, 1601, where his name was mistakenly entered in the hospital records as "Mils Stansen." Then, to complicate matters further, he is recorded as dying there twelve days later. How such an error occurred is explained by archivist, Dr. Jeremy Bangs, who believes that it was due to sloppy record keeping. He suggests that during this hectic battle period, there were tens of thousands of admissions, discharges and burials. He believes that Standish's discharge was mistakenly entered as a burial. (*)

When the war ended, young Standish remained behind on garrison duty. As part of a foreign community of about 4,000, it can be assumed that English countrymen would form relationships. For Myles, one of these may have been marriage to a Puritan lass that poets would later refer to as his "English Rose."

At any rate, we know that Standish did become acquainted with Puritan elders prior to 1620 and that he was invited to join them in a grand New World adventure. Apparently, he instructed at least some of them in the art of musketry before they left Leyden. William Bradford later wrote that a musket salute was part of the embarkation ceremony.

Chapter Eight

FINDING CAPTAIN MYLES STANDISH

LOATHE TO DEPART

With a limited budget, the Elders were restricted to only two modest ships. They chartered the Mayflower and purchased the smaller Speedwell. Neither vessel was anything special, but they were the best the Virginia Company would pay for and therefore would have to do.

The Mayflower was anchored in London and it was arranged that the Leideners would meet her there after crossing the Channel aboard the Speedwell. The old Mayflower was well past its prime, having been built thirty-two years earlier, in 1588. Its exact dimensions are unknown but naval historians believe her to be about one hundred feet overall, with a twenty-one foot beam. Heavily loaded, she would have ridden quite low in the water, drawing more than thirteen feet. This would prove to be a major drawback when the colonists later attempted to anchor in one of the typical natural, shallow harbors along the New England coastline.

Master Christopher Jones, skipper and part owner of the Mayflower, agreed to charter it to the Puritans for as long as it would take them to get established in the new Virginia Colony. The venerable old Speedwell was purchased outright by the Puritans and outfitted for the voyage by the London chandlers. Powder and heavy ordinance were loaded aboard, most certainly under the watchful eye of Myles Standish. (He did not yet hold the rank of captain.)

The Speedwell was considered especially crucial to the colony's trading success in the New World. With its smaller size and shallow draft, it would be ideal for fishing and trading along the Atlantic coast, their main endeavor. At the same time, the Speedwell was large enough to sail back to England whenever a cargo of furs was ready for shipment or when supplies from home base were needed.

Once they arrived in Virginia, the colonists planned to live aboard both vessels, using them as floating bases of operations, until suitable shelters could be built ashore. Because the possibility of Indian raids concerned them very much, living on the ships would avoid having to leave anyone behind while the rest were off trading or fishing; the lessons of Jamestown were still fresh in their minds.

The fact that none of them had any experience sailing a vessel of this size was not considered a problem; they would observe the sailors on the way over. They boarded the Speedwell at Delftshaven, a small port about 25 miles from Leyden.

The following may be the first time Bradford or anyone else uses the biblical word, "Pilgrim" to describe the Puritan émigrés. The term was picked up some time later by other writers and has since become commonly substituted for what they actually called themselves—
"Puritans."

Chapter Eight

FINDING CAPTAIN MYLES STANDISH

LOATHE TO DEPART

> And the time being come that they must depart, they were accompanied with most of their brethren out of the city into a town, sundry miles off, called Delftshaven, were the ship (Speedwell) lay ready to receive them. So they left that goodly and pleasant city which had been their resting place near twelve years; but they knew they were pilgrims, and looked not much on those things, but lift up their eyes to the heavens, their dearest country, and quieted their spirits. (2)

Pushed by "a prosperous winde," the Speedwell departed the Dutch coast, crossed the English Channel and sailed around the southern English coast past Portsmouth and into Southampton in only four days.

This first leg of their Atlantic crossing would prove to be just about the last of their good luck. It was not all their fault; it was the chandlers that failed them. When they landed in Southampton, the necessary supplies were supposed to be waiting dockside, ready to be put aboard ship, but they were not.

Much to their chagrin, they found that their agents had failed, for various petty reasons, to deliver as promised. It would be twenty more precious days before they could leave England; time they could not spare and could never make up.

It was during this time ashore in Southampton that the Puritan elders met the famous Captain John Smith who told them that for a consideration he would accompany them to New England. They declined; money was short, and besides, they already had his book and his maps. They also had their own military expert, Myles Standish, now a full partner in the enterprise.

Rather snidely, John Smith later wrote: "Their humorous ignorance caused them for more than a year to endure a wonderful deal of misery with infinite patience... thinking to find things better than I advised them." This is a perfect example of why Smith was perpetually in trouble with his employers and his peers; it had been his exaggerations that were mainly responsible for misleading the naive Leyden colonists to begin with.

Chapter Eight

FINDING CAPTAIN MYLES STANDISH

LOATHE TO DEPART

After more bickering among themselves and their agents, they finally came to terms. By August 5th, 1620, they had sold off enough of their butter supply and signed a letter of agreement that satisfied creditors and allowed them to continue their voyage. With high hopes well fortified by many devout prayers, they said farewell to new friends they had made while in port, hoisted anchor and set sail for Virginia, Captain Smith's promised land of milk and honey.

Before they had gone very far, Master Reynolds realized that the Speedwell was leaking profusely. He came about, signaled the Mayflower and consulted with Master Jones. They agreed that they would have to return to Dartmouth for emergency repairs. However, once there, no special leaks could be found. All agreed it was useless to try again, they were far behind schedule. Clearly, the skippers told them, the old Speedwell could not be made seaworthy due to "general weakness of the ship."

As critical as the Speedwell was to their long-range plans, they decided to go on without her. This decision would prove to be a serious mistake; they should have all turned back and waited until the following spring.

Later, some of the colonists would claim that Master Reynolds, regretting his commitment to remain an entire year with the colony, had deliberately mismanaged his ship. They said that he had purposely added too much sail, which separated the ship's planking, caused the leaks, and then gave him an excuse to escape his contract. They might be right; if his ship had been out of trim or under too great press of sail, an experienced skipper would have recognized it and known how to correct it.

---

* Author's note:

Fifty years after the Battle of Ostend, Myles, lying near death at his Duxbury home, concluded his last will with a bitter reference to how he had been cheated of his legal inheritance because of the erroneous report of his death in Holland. Isle of Man court documents confirm that, when word of Myles' supposed death reached the island, his brother William assumed control of the Standish estates and refused to relinquish them when Myles returned to claim his rightful inheritance.

Chapter Nine

FINDING CAPTAIN MYLES STANDISH

OLDE PONDE PLACE

THE MANSFIELD HISTORICAL SOCIETY

Strictly speaking, if we were going to follow the reverse sequence of our Standish ancestor's westward migration after they left Plymouth and Duxbury, our next stop would be Ashfield, not Mansfield. However, Mansfield is located in the east-central portion of Connecticut on a direct line to our Duxbury destination and we were urged by our hosts to arrive there in time for the 4th of July festivities. We planned to make Ashfield our final stop on the way home.

Several weeks before we left on our genealogical excursion, Elaine Corbett of the Duxbury Pilgrim Society suggested that I contact the Mansfield County Clerk to see if they would be willing to do a search for a Standish land purchase, circa 1735-40.

Our problem was that four generations of Standishes was as far as the Mayflower Society publication went. We were hoping to uncover more information about the Standish descendant that once lived in Mansfield; in order to establish whether they were part of our lineage. By careful analysis of all four-generation descendants, we were eventually able to narrow possibilities down to this particular Miles (there were many of them) and his son, Israel. We felt quite sure that this had to be the family line for which we were looking.

Chapter Nine

FINDING CAPTAIN MYLES STANDISH

OLDE PONDE PLACE

To my surprise and delight, my request to the Mansfield County Clerk's office hit pay dirt. Just before we embarked on our trip, I received two Standish land records; one of them was for Miles Standish's 1737 land purchase and the second was for its subsequent resale back to the original owner two years later. Miles was evidently not pleased with his purchase or perhaps he was persuaded by relatives living in Ashfield, Massachusetts that he would do better to join them there. Such a move would not have been decided upon lightly, Ashfield being located some one hundred miles northwest, a long journey by oxen-powered wagon.

We arrived in Mansfield in the early evening and had no trouble finding the town's Historical Society Museum, our goal for the next morning. It was located, as are many other New England museums, in the old town hall building. We were pleased to find that, even after all this time, Mansfield retains much of its historic, rural atmosphere (1990 population just 21,000). The first settlers came to the area about 1692, probably attracted by cheap, fertile land that was convenient to plenty of fresh water. Additionally, in a time and place where roads were practically non-existent, rivers and creeks were essential for transportation of goods too bulky or heavy to be toted on one's back or carried by a packhorse.

Preliminary research had informed us that one of the local lowland areas was known as Mansfield Hollow; another was called Olde Ponde Place. Several creeks and rivers not only made getting there more convenient, they provided the power necessary to run the saw mills and grist mills vital to frontier commerce and development.

By the time Captain Myles' great-grandson Miles, (note spelling variation) came to Mansfield, it was still on the frontier and sparsely populated, but with so many natural advantages it must have looked to Miles like an ideal place to settle. Even so, there were many things for the settlers to worry about; the dislocated Indian tribes not the least of them. The French and the British were still contesting possession of all territory west of the Allegheny Mountains, a continuing dispute that, fifteen years in the future, would erupt into the bloody seven-year French and Indian Wars. It was also about this time that a twenty-two year-old George Washington began his military career as a staff officer in the Colonial British Army.

The next morning, while on an early walk through the village, I exchanged pleasantries with a distinguished, older woman (about my age) tending flowers in her yard just a few doors from the Historical Society building. On a hunch, I asked if she might be Roberta Smith, the person I had come to Mansfield to see. By a happy coincidence, she said she indeed was. I had telephoned her several weeks earlier, explained my mission and was pleased to find that she was eager to assist me in any way she could, however she said she had never heard of any Standishes living in early Mansfield.

Chapter Nine

FINDING CAPTAIN MYLES STANDISH

OLDE PONDE PLACE

I was very pleased to present Miss Smith with several documents I had just received from the local County Clerk's office. I gave her copies of two ancient Standish land records. In 1737, a Miles Standish had purchased property from an early Mansfield pioneer, William Huntington, a name with which Miss Smith was quite familiar. The second document recorded the sale of the same property back to the original owner just two years later, in 1739.

The old quill-written script was hard to read and, for me, impossible to understand. Miss Smith, a retired university librarian and lifelong scholar in such matters, believed she could decipher the old script but said it would take some time to accomplish. Of course, I told her to take all the time she needed. Obviously, I had found just the right person at the right time.

The document shown on the following pages has been digitally modified for readability but serves to illustrate Roberta's patience and skill in deciphering such documents. Except for the central area of the page, which I left as it was, I carefully removed most of the ink splotches in order to make it at least partially legible to ordinary mortals. Most, but fortunately not all, of the landmarks referred to by the 1772 surveyor had long since disappeared. It was not unusual for surveyors of that era to reference a certain pile of rocks, a pine stump and, in one case, a white oak bush. Although Roberta had warned us that it would probably not be possible to identify the exact location of the Standish property, we hoped for the best and waited for her to work her magic—she being almost as excited as we were.

In a matter of hours, Roberta reported that one of the very first surveyor reference points mentioned in the Standish land purchase still existed! It began at "a pile of stones on a side hill, which lies towards and near a Large Pond." Roberta reminded us (we were by now on a first name basis), that early settlers had named their community "Ponde Place," the forerunner of present-day Mansfield. Since this distinctive pond was now a focal point of a nearby lake, it presented the unmistakable beginning surveying point of the Standish purchase.

Roberta also explained that the mentioned Nachauge Swamp is still known by that name and that when combined with the deed's other reference to a "Large Pond," it was now possible to locate the Standish-Huntington property within a matter of yards. Elated at this news, Roberta, Ruth and I set out in our rental car to see it for ourselves. Guided by Roberta, we drove to historic Nachauge Swamp and were pleased to see that the old swamp has been converted to the beautiful Mansfield Hollow State Park. Due to the peaceful, serene beauty of the setting, we were not at all disappointed to learn that most, if not all, of the old Standish property is now under water as is part of a much-needed flood-control project and the park itself. As part of the park development, a substantial concrete dam controls floodwaters from two adjoining rivers that meet nearby, the Mt. Hope and the Fenton.

Chapter Nine

FINDING CAPTAIN MYLES STANDISH

OLDE PONDE PLACE

After parking in the visitor parking lot we climbed a set of some fifty or so rather steep steps leading up to the top of a substantial concrete dam. Once there, we were happy to see a beautiful, five-hundred acre lake, created by the dam on which we stood. This lake, we later learned, was called Naubesatuck, the original Indian name for the Mansfield Center area.

The lake is relatively shallow, the water fresh and pure. No swimming is permitted, however. The lake supplies drinking water to nearby Willimantic city. A variety of sailboats and canoes could be seen as well as anglers trying their luck. Just below the dam, several fishermen in hip boots were fly-casting for trout in the fast moving spillway.

Mansfield Hollow State Park Dam

Our park guidebook contained a map with an overview of the park on which I, with Roberta Smith's guidance, placed an "X" to mark the approximate site of our likely (we were still not sure of our relationship) Standish ancestor's home. According to the old deed, Miles' home was located on the edge of the pond now called Echo Lake, quite near the dam. We could not be exact, of course, but there was no need to be too precise. Without doubt, Miles had lived within the sound of our voice.

Chapter Nine

FINDING CAPTAIN MYLES STANDISH

OLDE PONDE PLACE

Later, back at the Historical Society, Roberta showed us the portion of the Standish land purchase document that enabled her to locate, with reasonable precision, just where the Standish property had lain. Although most of the referenced landmarks quoted by the surveyor no longer exist, she found two unmistakable reference points in the old deed that were still identifiable. The original wording quoted below is as it was written, in one long, convoluted, single sentence:

> "Beginning at a heap of Stones from thence the Line Runs Easterly thirty-nine rods & 20 links to a heap of Stones from thence the line Runs north 36 (degrees) 30 (minutes) north ten rods & 12 Links to a branch marked which Stands at the South Easterly Corner of said Pond from thence the Line Runs fifteen rods & 18 Links to a branch Stake marked Standing the South Side of said pond from thence the Line Runs by said pond Westerly, Six rods & Six Links to a white oak bush marked from thence the Line runs north westerly Twenty one Rods from thence northerly thirty-three rods & 7 Links to a heap of Stones & a white oak Stake marked TH being the north East Corner then Running west 28 (degrees) 30 (minutes) S six Rods & 20 Links to a pine Stub then Running Southerly twenty four rods & 14 Links to a heap of Stones by the path that goeth to Nachauge Swamp . . ."

The following document is not the actual Standish land purchase agreement but it is quite similar and is shown here to give the reader an idea of what Miss Smith had to work with. The original Standish document was in even worse condition and I could not face the prospect of digitally removing all the ink splotches from another such paper.

Chapter Nine

FINDING CAPTAIN MYLES STANDISH

OLDE PONDE PLACE

Chapter Nine

FINDING CAPTAIN MYLES STANDISH

OLDE PONDE PLACE

August, 1990

Dear Mr. Haviland,

I have started transcribing the deeds for you, but ran into a number of snags. Also, part of the first deed from Huntington to Standish is missing, there should be another page or part of a page, crucial because it is the conclusion and lists the exact date of the transaction.

I went to check the original deed to see if I could puzzle out the problems. Unfortunately, the town clerk has sent the volume to be treated and rebound. This is to alert you of a possible long delay as it will probably not be returned for several months. Meanwhile I have puzzled out enough to determine more accurately the location. One of the boundaries is the east side of the Great Pond, which shows on the map. It was quite exciting for me, as this is very close to, if not part of the land we have been fighting to save from an unwelcome development.

Roberta K. Smith

August 1990

Dear Mr. Haviland:

The Land Record volume returned sooner than expected, enabling me to complete the transcribing. It was a very slow process due to Clerk Thomas Storrs difficult handwriting. You will note I transcribed as he wrote, with lack of punctuation and with typical spelling of the period. The few question marks here and there are words I could not puzzle

Chapter Nine

FINDING CAPTAIN MYLES STANDISH

OLDE PONDE PLACE

out. You will note the two deeds are quite consistent, the dimensions especially. I was puzzled about the location of the cedar swamp until I noted in the first deed the clerk added the word Nachauge which is a real clue. This swamp was probably in the vicinity of the present dam either below or above it. Also, it was indeed exciting to be able to pinpoint the rest of the acreage, all east of Echo Pond. Mansfield was originally called Pond Place by the earliest settlers, after this very pond. Later it was called Town Pond and I do wish they had retained that name. The maps indicate the general location. Part of this is owned by Joshua's Tract Conservation and Historic Trust Inc., a land preservation group we are very proud of. Doesn't that please you to know this land is preserved? Sometime in the future I hope you may have the opportunity to take a walk on the trails.

There is no indication of a dwelling on the property in these deeds, so we cannot determine were Miles lived. However, he was certainly a resident of Mansfield as is noted in the first deed. Also, I located when he joined First Church, here in Mansfield, in 1738.

Xerox enclosed. Was Miles the grandson of Capt. Myles Standish? We would like this information for our Society records.

Best wishes to you and Mrs. Haviland,
Roberta K Smith

Author's Note: Advised her he was a Great Grandson.

Chapter Ten

FINDING CAPTAIN MYLES STANDISH

The Crossing

The Mayflower (artist rendition)

They were a youthful group—of the forty-four male colonists aboard, just two were over the age of fifty and only nine were past forty. Still, age was important. Very few of the over-thirty group would survive the first terrible winter ashore. Myles Standish was thirty-six; John Allenton, thirty-two; William Bradford, thirty-one; Gilbert Winslow, twenty-five; and John Alden twenty-one. In time, these men would become known as the Pilgrim Fathers. There were nineteen adult women.

The William Mullins family boarded the Mayflower at London, along with their two children, Joseph and Priscilla. With them was Joseph Carter, a servant. With the exception of Priscilla, all would be dead within the next few months. She alone, of her family would survive. She eventually wed John Alden and bore him eleven children. Young Alden was not recruited until the Speedwell was undergoing repairs at Dartmouth. Belatedly, they realized that they would soon need quantities of wooden barrels and a skilled cooper to make them. Initially Alden signed on for three years but he would continue with them as a valued, well-liked member of the colony. He, Myles, and their families would become lifelong friends.

Chapter Ten

FINDING CAPTAIN MYLES STANDISH

The Crossing

Although none of them were anything approaching wealthy, quite a few of them took servants. Eleven of the eighteen indentured servants were young children. Without a public education system, it was common practice for children to be bound to a master for a period of seven years in which they were furnished food, clothing and housing while being taught reading and writing along with a craft or trade. Four of the bound children were poorhouse orphans.

Like most merchant ships of its day, the Mayflower had a high forecastle and poop deck. When loaded heavily, the decks in the middle part of the ship rode quite low in the water. When quartering the wind in rough seas, waves washed continuously over the deck, making them wet and dangerous. Salt water sloshed freely below deck, keeping everyone damp and miserable. During most of the voyage, passengers were allowed topside only briefly, if at all.

The below-deck headroom space was barely five and one-half feet at mid-deck, much less near the sides. They took no cattle along this voyage but may have had poultry, pigs and perhaps goats. Furniture would have taken up too much valuable space but they did bring along wood for furniture making. Stowed in every nook and cranny were pewter household utensils, candle molds and trinkets for later trade with the "savages," as they all called them.

Allowing for the space reserved for captain and crew, each passenger had an average of about 3 x 6 feet, hardly room enough to sleep, cook, play or be sick in. They took with them such staples as bacon, hard tack, salt beef, cheese, salted fish, various dried fruits, butter, vinegar and mustard. The ship's hold contained many stout barrels of salt, an absolute necessity—with no refrigeration, salting or smoking was the only reliable method of preserving meat.

Citizens of the Elizabethan period regarded water with suspicion and for good reason; it was seldom pure, usually foul, and best used sparingly. Even at London's royal court, bathing was considered unhealthy and drinking the stuff was avoided if fermented beer could be had. Somewhat surprisingly, the Puritans, generally opposed to anything remotely pleasurable, did not regard the moderate use of alcohol as being sinful. They found room for substantial quantities of "beare" and "hard water," probably brandy. The Puritan "hard water' packed a wallop. Months later when they offered some to a visiting Indian dignitary, he took a large swallow and immediately broke out in a heavy sweat, greatly amusing them all. This incident may have led to the first use of the term, "firewater."

The colonists' gunpowder supply appears to have been quite plentiful. Even after they had gotten themselves well settled onshore and had become concerned about hostile Indians, Standish never skimped on the use of powder. This was evident by the way he trained the Puritans in musketry and the fact that ceremonial volleys were fired on all sorts of public occasions. It also served another purpose; it greatly impressed the local Indians.

Chapter Ten

FINDING CAPTAIN MYLES STANDISH

The Crossing

For the first half of the voyage, good weather and fair winds favored the Mayflower. Then, it being so late in the season, the usual rough autumn weather caught up with them. The rest of the trip was a landlubber's nightmare.

> After they had enjoyed fair winds and weather for a season they ..."met with many fierce storms, with which the ship was shroudly (severely) shaken, and her beams in the mid-ships was bowed and cracked, which put them in some fear that the ship could not be able to perform the voyage." (2)

The integrity of the beam was crucial. It had to be repaired quickly or the ship was sure to break up in the choppy seas. They had no replacement, but from somewhere in the hold, probably cannibalized from a printing press, a large jackscrew was found and used to force the cracked beam back into position where it was mended and reinforced. It was about this time that some of the more superstitious sailors became alarmed and in various ways, subtle and direct, let the passengers know that they thought they ought to turn back to England.

> ... of the company, perceiving the mariners to fear the sufficiency of the ship, as appeared by their muttering, they entered into serious consultation with the Master and other officers of the ship, to consider in time of the danger; and rather to return then to cast themselves into a desperate and inevitable peril. And truly there was great distraction and difference of opinion amongst the mariners themselves; fain would they do what could be done for their wages sake, (being now half-seas over, and on the other hand they were loath to hazard their lives too desperately. (2)

As military advisor, Standish must have been involved in this debate, but Bradford does not mention it. We do not know how Standish argued but, not being a timid man; it is hard to imagine him voting to turn back with the voyage "half-seas over." Master Christopher Jones, doubtless aware that he would not be paid if he failed to fulfill his promise to deliver them in New England, ordered 'steady helm'. They sailed on, but not without strong misgivings on the part of the ship's sailors and seasick passengers.

Chapter Ten

FINDING CAPTAIN MYLES STANDISH

The Crossing

> So they committed themselves to the will of God, and resolved to proceed. In sundry of these storms, the winds were so fierce, and the seas so high, as they could not bear a knot of sails, but were forced to hull (drift sans sails) for diverse days together. (2)

Hatches were tightly secured in rough weather, as were portholes, shutting out fresh air; sun and sky. Passengers were seldom allowed topside, as the wet, slippery decks were treacherous even for experienced sailors. The steady pitching and yawing of the heavily laden ship, although constant, was tolerable in good weather, horrible when seas were high. For endless days and nights, they had to brace themselves to avoid jostling each other or to keep from being slammed against heaving bulkheads. The working of the ship's ancient joints, the creaking of her beams and the endless smashing of wave after wave mingled with cries of injured children and moans of seasick passengers were unrelenting. They ate when they could, mostly cold rations; starting even a small cooking fire in a wooden ship was much too risky.

Sometime during the voyage, probably near the end, Elizabeth Hopkins gave birth to a son which they named Oceanus. Sadly, the littlest Pilgrim did not survive to see his first birthday. But, there was one thing they all could be thankful for: the deepest recess of a ship's hold normally sloshes with foul-smelling bilge water, but the Mayflower's was not all that bad. They had selected her partly because of her reputation as being a "sweet" ship due to the wine cargoes she had specialized in transporting.

By the time Bradford wrote his journal some twenty years later; the memory of all this seems to have faded. He barely mentions it. Perhaps the memories of the crossing had simply faded into insignificance; so much worse had happened since then. This may account for the fact that, in spite of a long and rough crossing, only one, a young sailor, died en route. Actually, the sailor's death should not be charged against the ship. He took sick and died suddenly from a mysterious illness shortly before landfall. The obnoxious lad was little mourned by the Puritans. He had been quite mean to all of them, gleefully informing them that before the voyage was over, he would be tossing many of their bodies into the deep.

The Puritans righteously agreed that the troublesome sailor's death was God's punishment on their behalf. They cheerfully helped with the sea burial, pleased to assist the Lord with his good works. It is not certain just what it was that the sailors, and then the passengers, began dying of. Six took sick and expired within a month. It was probably a plague picked up by the sailor back in England. He may have had his final revenge when he passed the disease on to his pallbearers as they tossed him over the side.

Chapter Ten

FINDING CAPTAIN MYLES STANDISH

The Crossing

There was much excitement aboard the Mayflower when a pod of sounding whales was spotted nearby. Everyone able to do so, went topside to admire them. When sailors told them that the whale oil from just one large creature was worth three or four thousand pounds, some of the passengers wished they had taken harpoons along, naively thinking taking a whale would have been possible for them to do.

> November 9, 1620 - After many difficulties in boisterous storms, at length by God's good providence we espied land, the appearance of it much comforted us, especially seeing so goodly a land and wooded to the brink of the sea. It caused us to rejoice together and praise God that had given us once again to see land. (2)

Land Ho! At the long-awaited cry from the masthead lookout, excited passengers dashed cheering to the rail, shouting thanks to God for their deliverance. But the jubilation ceased abruptly when some of the sailors reluctantly told them that they recognized the shoreline and it was definitely not the mouth of the Hudson where they were supposed to be; they were nowhere near the land specified by the King's charter. Reluctantly, Jones admitted he had landed them at Cape Cod, hundreds of miles from where they should have been; it was the Atlantic storms, he argued; poor navigation had nothing to do with it. They were anchored in a fine harbor but it was not where they were supposed to be; the King's charter was very specific.

Chapter Ten

FINDING CAPTAIN MYLES STANDISH

The Crossing

Even so, Jones then urged the colonists to stay where they were; he was anxious to put his passengers ashore, refurbish his ship and head back to London before the weather worsened, or his provisions gave out. "Yea, it was muttered by some that if they got not a lace in time, they would turn them and their goods ashore and leave them," said Bradford in his journal.

As they always did whenever a decision was required, the soon-to-be colonists discussed their options at length and voted to take on wood and fresh water and then sail on to Virginia as the King's charter specified. Master Jones was not very happy at this, but the Saints insisted and he reluctantly agreed to set them down in Virginia as his contract dictated.

Relocating was easier said than done. Stiff December winds were against them and, after several hours of fruitless tacking, they found themselves in shallow water surrounded by dangerous shoals. With great difficulty, Jones extricated the ship from a near catastrophe. There was no dissent when he set sail to go back to the safe harbor they had just left. The Mayflower passengers longed to walk upon solid ground and were eager to quit the ship. Having spent eight weeks jammed together below decks while the ship unceasingly bounced upon rough seas had been a nightmare. Rations were also scant and the thought of sailing for weeks more in order to get to Virginia was more than they could bear, charter or no.

Jones again cautioned the elders that at this time of year, contrary winds would require him to spend weeks tacking into strong headwinds. They would have to sail back and forth many hundreds of miles out to sea in order to reach their Virginia destination. The thought of this horrified them sufficiently so that when Jones repeated his recommendation that they spend the winter at Cape Cod, they changed their minds. Provisions were running low and, besides, they had serious sickness aboard.

From the very first, there had been a troublesome division amongst the passengers due in part to the Puritans habit of referring to themselves as "Saints," and everyone else as "Strangers." Quite understandably, this attitude had been much resented. Shortly after the ship came about and returned to its former anchorage, a group of dissatisfied "Strangers" informed the Puritan elders that things were going to change; since they were no longer going to Virginia as specified by the King's charter, they would no longer permit the Puritans to order them about.

This unwelcome announcement came as a bombshell. Goodwill and cooperation were necessary or the colony would fall apart even before it began. Because of his military background, it was probably Standish who best understood the threat of rebellion in the ranks and urged them to take strong and decisive corrective action. He would have known that the Puritans were at their strongest while still aboard ship where Jones and his men could back them up if it became necessary.

Chapter Ten

FINDING CAPTAIN MYLES STANDISH

The Crossing

Exactly what methods or words of persuasion were employed by the Saints to bring the mutinous rebel Strangers into line, is not mentioned by Bradford. He merely states that by the time they anchored that evening, every adult male on board had signed what has since become known as the Mayflower Covenant. That this remarkable document could be crafted aboard a tossing ship, in a rough ocean, in a matter of just a few hours, challenges credulity.

They were all accustomed to long debates about anything and everything they did. Now that the mutinous "Strangers" were included, they surely would have insisted on being heard as well. Ordinary folk of that era could seldom do more than write their names and perhaps read their bible, but all were able to speak their minds and regularly did so. Historians have suggested that the actual writing of the Covenant was probably a joint effort by Bradford and Carver, with suggestions from others. But, such a smooth melding of strong opinions seems quite out of character. There is no way to prove or disprove this as the actual Mayflower document does not exist. Like many of the colonists, it did not survive the first winter ashore. Bradford's version of this historic agreement was not set down again until he wrote his memoirs some 20 years later, by which time John Carver was long gone. William may have polished it up a bit and doubtlessly made sure that everyone aboard the Mayflower "signed" it. Most of them, like John Carver, were no longer alive.

One can only imagine the discussion that took place when drafting this historic agreement; they would have been anxious to set foot on dry land. It is interesting to note that, some one hundred and twenty-five years later, this covenant would serve as the basis for the Bill of Rights; the cornerstone of the United States Constitution.

The Mayflower Covenant (*)
11 November 1620

Having undertaken for the glory of God, and advancement of the Christian faith, and honor of our King and Country, a Voyage to plant the first Colony in the Northern parts of Virginia, do by these presents solemnly and mutually covenant and combine ourselves together into a civil body politic for our better ordering and preservation, and furtherance of the ends aforesaid; and by virtue hereof to enact, constitute, and frame such just and equal Laws, Ordinances, acts constitutions, & offices from time to time as shall be thought most meet and convenient for the general good of the Colony; unto which we promise all due submission and obedience.

LOOKING FOR CAPTAIN MYLES STANDISH

The Crossing

Chapter Ten

John Carver - William Bradford - Edward Winslow - William Brewster
Isaac Allerton - Myles Standish - John Alden - John Turner - Francis Eaton
James Chilton - John Craxton - John Billington - Moses Fletcher
John Goodman - Samuel Fuller - Christopher Martin - William Mullins
William White - Richard Warren - John Howland - Stephen Hopkins
Digery Priest - -Thomas Williams - Gilbert Winslow - Edmund Margesson
Peter Brown - Richard Britteridge - George Soule - Edward Tilly
John Tilly - Francis Cooke - Thomas Rogers - Thomas Tinker
John Ridgdale - Edward Fuller - Richard Clark - Richard Gardiner
Mr. John Allerton - Thomas English - Edward Doten

After dispensing with this critical piece of business, they focused on other matters. Their first venture ashore was taken sixty-five days after leaving England, on November 11th, 1620. They tacked around the northern tip of Cape Cod and anchored on a broad sandy beach just south of present-day Provincetown. The better known, more historic Plymouth Rock landing would not take place for another month, if then (more about that later). As soon as the ship was secure, the people went ashore to shake off the months of travel, to wash their linen and to explore what they perceived to be an uninhabited wilderness.

William Bradford compiled his memoirs some twenty years after the events took place and are, therefore, subject to a certain amount of healthy skepticism. This seems especially true of his recollection of what was an extremely contentious, near-rebellion aboard the Mayflower.

 Author's note: The passengers listed above are supposed to have signed the Mayflower Compact but we cannot be sure of this; the original of the document does not exist, apparently lost during the travails of the colonists' early years at Plymouth. What we do have is William Bradford's best recollection of what the Compact itself contained and those who were its signatories.

Chapter Eleven

FINDING CAPTAIN MYLES STANDISH

THE FIRST EXPEDITIONS

A shallow draft shallop

Before leaving England, a shallop had been purchased, disassembled and stowed deep in the Mayflower's hold. Its shallow draft made it ideal for entering unimproved harbors. It could carry a dozen passengers or, as they hoped, a half-dozen men and a large cargo of valuable furs.

However, during the crossing, some of the passengers surreptitiously borrowed several sections of the boat for use as a platform for their bed, causing the planks to warp. When the pieces were removed and taken ashore, the warped planks no longer fit properly. After soaking the planks in hot water, the carpenters were, with difficulty, able to reshape them to make a proper watertight fit. A task that should have been completed in less than four days, took sixteen.

Rather than waste valuable time waiting for the shallop to be repaired and reassembled, on November 15, Standish took sixteen armed men on a land reconnaissance along the near coastline. They hoped to contact some of the local natives and perhaps make friends with them.

Chapter Eleven

FINDING CAPTAIN MYLES STANDISH

THE FIRST EXPEDITIONS

The explorers soon saw some Indians from afar, but were unable to catch up with them. Looking around, they discovered a cache of Indian corn buried in an iron kettle. They must have known, or at least suspected, that both items were extremely valuable in the local native culture—especially the iron kettle—but they took it with them anyway, assuring one another that they would later compensate the tribesmen for what they had taken. The Indians, of course, had no way of knowing this, but it should have occurred to the colonists, that to appropriate these items on their first visit ashore was not a good way to make friends. Instead, they regarded it as a gift from God.

> And here it to be noticed a special providence of God, and a great mercy to this poor people, that here they got seed to plant them corn the next year or else they might have starved, for they had none, nor any likelihood to get any till the season had been past as the sequel did manifest (as events showed). But the Lord is never wanting unto His in their greatest needs: let his holy name have all the praise! (2)

Abandoned Pamet dwelling

Chapter Eleven

FINDING CAPTAIN MYLES STANDISH

THE FIRST EXPEDITIONS

They would eventually learn that the corn belonged to the Pamet Indians, a minor sub-tribe of the vast Algonquin Nation. A few years earlier, a severe plague, brought from Europe by traders or sailors, had very nearly wiped out the entire tribe; so few survivors remained, that no one was left to work the fields. Entire villages were abandoned. These were the people the Pilgrims hoped would be willing to trade food and furs for trinkets.

It is ever thus: When an advanced culture meets a lesser one, it is always the more primitive people that suffer.

The reader may well wonder how it was that these Puritans, many of them farmers, had come to the New World without a supply of seed corn of their own. The answer is simple; in all likelihood, few, if any of them had ever seen it before. Maize was first developed in Central America and over many centuries its use spread gradually into Native North America.

They found many game trails, but no Indians. A good laugh was had by all when William Bradford was left dangling in the air after stepping in the camouflaged noose of an Indian's snare trap set in hopes of catching a passing deer.

The shallop was finally made seaworthy on the 26th of November. It was fitted with sails and necessary nautical gear and pronounced ready for duty. But first, another conference was held, at which they decided to go back along the shore they had earlier reconnoitered on foot for a further look. Some of the fresh water creeks they had seen emptying into the ocean looked promising as a place for them to build permanent habitation.

Master Jones, now resigned to over-wintering with the colonists, was anxious to find a harbor where his precious ship would be secure from winter storms. He offered to join the expedition and bring nine sailors and one of the ship's boats with him. "We made Master Jones our leader, for we thought it best herein to gratify his kindness and forwardness." (2)

Chapter Eleven

FINDING CAPTAIN MYLES STANDISH

THE FIRST EXPEDITIONS

Selecting Jones to lead them was courteous, but most unwise. He was not at all familiar with the terrain and lacked Standish's experience in land reconnaissance and warding off enemy attacks, should they occur. Also, an affront such as this would not have set well with any military man, especially one with a temper. However, this seems not to have occurred to the Puritan Elders; Jones was their man. They were used to discussing and voting on anything and everything the group did, so it did not seem to matter much who "led" them.

They soon found another grave, this one obviously a person of importance. Casting aside earlier principles forbidding "odious ransacking of sepulchers, they digged it up and found broaches and combs along with a great many bowles, trayes, dishes and such like trinkets."

Not satisfied with this, ". . . at length we came to a fair new Indian mat, beneath which were two bundles, the one bigger, the other less." They opened the larger of the two and discovered the skull and bones of a man who had been liberally sprinkled with red ochre, a well-known sign of status. Then they were further amazed to realize that they had uncovered the grave of what was obviously a white man!

> The skull had fine yellow hair still on it, and some of the flesh unconsumed; there was bound up with a knife, a packneedle and two or three old iron things bound up in a sailors canvas shirt. Also a pair of cloth breeches; the red powder was a kind of embalmment, and yielded a strong, but not offensive smell; It was as fine as any flower. (3)

Upon opening the smaller bundle they saw ". . .the bones and head of a little child, about the legs and about other parts of it was bound strings, and bracelets of fine white beads; there was also by it a little bow, about three quarters long, and some other child's trinkets."

> "There was a variety of opinion amongst us about the embalmed person. Some thought it was an Indian lord and king; others said that the Indians all have black hair and never was seen with brown or yellow hair. Some thought it was a Christian of special note who had died amongst them and they buried him this to honor him. Others thought they had killed him and had done it in triumph over him." They covered up the graves, more respectfully now but they still took "sundry of the prettiest things away with us". (2)

Chapter Eleven

FINDING CAPTAIN MYLES STANDISH

THE FIRST EXPEDITIONS

They went back and continued along the beach but six inches of fresh snow made it tough going. The snow was crusty, but not strong enough to support the weight of a man. "Master Jones was wearied with marching and desirous that we should take up our lodging, though some of us would have marched further."

Bradford is tactful concerning the Mayflower skipper being unable to keep up with the men he was supposed to lead. They would have preferred to continue looking for a more protected place to camp but instead had to accommodate Master Jones by stopping early to make camp in the worst exposed place imaginable.

However, the campsite seemed much improved after several of the better marksmen knocked down three fat geese along with a half dozen ducks that were promptly cooked over a driftwood fire. They dined under fragrant pines. Bradford recalls the event with considerable relish: ". . . we ate with soldiers' stomachs, for we had eaten little all that day."

> "They could not go on coasting and discovery without danger of losing both men and boat, especially considering what variable winds and sudden storms do there arise. Upon this would follow the overthrow of all. Also cold and wet lodging had so tainted our people as scarce any of them were free from vehement coughs. If they should continue long in that estate it would endanger the lives of many and breed diseases and infection among us." (2)

Soaked to the skin from the freezing surf, they decided to march on and leave Master Jones and the shallop crew behind; they would catch up as soon as the weather permitted. The marchers made painfully slow progress in the soft sand, hiking no more than six or seven miles before nightfall. They spent a miserable night in the open with no dry blankets and no fire. "It blowed and did snowed all that day and night and froze withal. Some of our people that are dead took the original of their death there," Bradford sadly recalls.

The weather improved slightly the next day, the 27th of November. Before noon, Jones and his crew caught up to the exhausted, half-frozen marchers. They tumbled into the open shallop as the sailors set course for the Pamet River that they had noted earlier. In memory of the miserable night they had just spent, they named their overnight campsite Cold Harbor, a name that survives to this day.

Chapter Eleven

FINDING CAPTAIN MYLES STANDISH

THE FIRST EXPEDITIONS

Master Jones took one of the boats back to the Mayflower loaded with several sick crewmembers, along with their plundered Indian corn. The rest of them took up spades and mattocks and set off to make contact with the Indians. Bradford does not mention the purpose of the digging tools but there can be only one conclusion—they planned to loot more graves.

The fishing nearby appeared promising and they saw whales sounding just offshore. The harbor appeared adequate for smaller boats, though unsuitable for larger ships. The site was judged "healthful, secure and defensible." By far the most convincing argument for choosing this site was the lack of time. Winter was upon them and the weather would soon get worse. The deaths aboard the Mayflower were becoming more and more alarming. At first, it was just a few, but now they were occurring in ever-increasing numbers.

There was one happy event about this time; Susannah White gave birth to a son, the first Englishman to be born in New England. Mrs. White selected thoughtfully, naming her son Peregrine, "One who is a Pilgrim." His father died soon after the little fellow was born.

Chapter Twelve

FINDING CAPTAIN MYLES STANDISH

The First Encounter

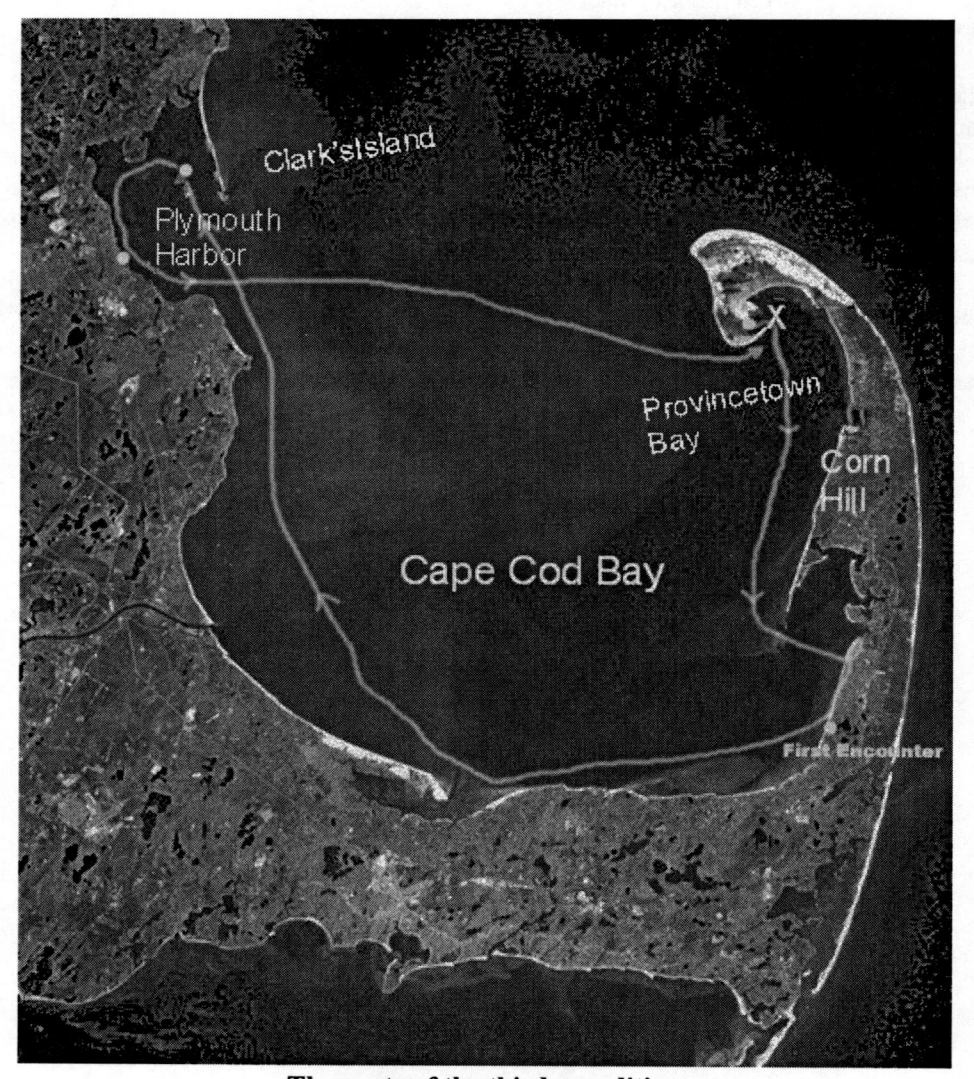

The route of the third expedition

Chapter Twelve

FINDING CAPTAIN MYLES STANDISH

The First Encounter

As always, some were not quite ready to make a final decision. They argued that they had not yet looked at all the habitation possibilities; for all they knew, there might be a superior one close by. Others recalled how Captain John Smith had told them of a particularly good harbor across the bay on the mainland which he christened after his favorite English city, Plymouth.

Anyway, the site they were considering would require water to be carried up a long, steep hill; for the women this was a definite minus. The womenfolk did not have a vote in such matters, but they probably expressed their objections to their husbands in private. It would be up to the women to fetch the water.

Drinking the water that had been stored on board ship was avoided whenever possible. It was known to be the principal cause of many serious stomach ailments. Even the children were encouraged to slack their thirst with fermented beer, a much healthier beverage since the fermentation process "purified the beare." Now, it was almost gone. Things were getting serious.

Wednesday, the sixth of December, 1620. It was resolved our discoverers should set forth . . . So ten of our men were appointed who were of themselves willing to undertake it, to wit, Captain Standish, Master Carver, William Bradford, Edward Winslow, John Tilley, Edward Tilley, John Howland, and three of London, Richard Warren, Stephen Hopkins and Edward Doten, and two of our seamen, John Alderton, and Thomas English. Of the ship's company there went two of the master's mates, Master Clarke and Master Coppin, the master gunner, and three sailors . . . (2, 14)

Once the decision was made to go on one more brief exploration, high winds and rough seas made it impossible for them to leave the Mayflower, but the next day it improved slightly. Although the weather was still terrible, they knew it would only get worse. Winter was closing in. The "Sickness" was spreading and the ranks of the able-bodied were thinning. More were dying every week; action was required.

Chapter Twelve

FINDING CAPTAIN MYLES STANDISH

The First Encounter

Standish took with him six Saints and four Strangers along with six sailors from the Mayflower. He planned to follow the inside Cape shore and then continue west across the southern shore and head north until a suitable colony site could be found. All of them realized that the deteriorating weather would make it a difficult mission, but it turned out to be far worse than anyone anticipated.

Salt water spray blasted over the shallop's bow, drenching them to the skin. The ice-laden sail was impossible to raise in the gusty wind. After leaving the Mayflower, they bent their backs to the oars, rowing landward, hoping that the wind would ease once they came closer to the Cape shore. Their salt-glazed clothes fit them "like coates of iron." Rowing furiously to keep the bow pointed into the wind, lest they be broadsided by a wave and capsized, they eventually came closer to shore and calmer waters. The ice holding the canvas to the boom was chipped loose and slowly the stubborn canvas was forced up the mast.

Once the sail was up and sheets secured, Mate Robert Coffin swung the tiller hard over to catch the wind, forgetting about the extra weight of the ice on the mast and sails. Slowly the vessel backed off the wind then suddenly heeled so smartly that the port side oarlocks shipped water, very nearly capsizing. Slowly, the shallop gained way, picking up speed on a broad reach that took them southerly, parallel to the inside Cape shoreline.

As soon as they had stopped rowing, they froze to the planks upon which they sat. With numb hands stuffed inside their coats, they huddled, backs to the wind, waiting, enduring. They recognized Corn Hill, perhaps guiltily remembering how they had "borrowed" an Indian's cache of seed corn and reminding each other how they were going to pay for it in the spring.

The shallop sped south through calm waters for an hour, then another, holding course parallel to the beach. They kept close enough to inspect shoreline features, but far enough out to avoid shoals. No river, creek or harbor presented itself that looked suitable for a new colony. Several passed out from the cold. Edward Tilley suffered the most. He would survive this day but would be dead from its effects within the month.

Eventually they came to a broad bay that they named "Wellfleet," as it is still known. It was far from what they had in mind but they had to go ashore or perish from the cold. While maneuvering landward, small clusters of Indians were seen around a large, black object on the beach, too far away to identify. The shallop was finally brought ashore several miles from where the Indians had been. They dragged the ice-laden craft far enough up the dunes to be safe from high tide. Curious to see what the Indians had been up to and hopeful of making useful contact, they hiked back north, extremely glad of the blood-warming exercise.

Chapter Twelve

FINDING CAPTAIN MYLES STANDISH

The First Encounter

They found a large black fish of the porpoise family that had washed up on the beach, a grampus, about fifteen feet long. The Indians were gone. After searching in the woods until dark, the exhausted men gathered enough pine branches and driftwood to make a blazing fire and a crude barricade to protect against the wind—and any nearby hostile natives.

At last, they were able to warm their numb fingers over the welcome fire. Clothing was spread to dry and meager rations were heated and quickly devoured. A flask of hard water would have been most welcome but they had none.

Another campfire could be seen glowing in the darkness several miles farther up the beach, Realizing it had to be the Indians they had seen earlier, Standish organized a night guard and took the first watch himself. Each man dug a shallow depression in the sand, arranged their still-damp blankets as best they could and settled in for a long, cold, miserable, but hopefully, uneventful night. The next morning, Standish had his fellows marching out of camp at first light. Edward Tilley and several others too sick to continue were left behind with the shallop.

Several more grampuses were found washed up on shore and stranded on the ice. Bradford states that the fish were five or six paces long. Using a sharp cutlass to open one of them, they were surprised and pleased to see how fat it was. Oil was an important commodity, always in short supply, and this was "some 2 inches thicke of fat like a hog, and fleshed like swine."

Disabled companions were carried back through the surf and placed aboard the shallop after which they sailed the short distance back to Wellfleet Bay. The Indians had been back, obviously hoping to claim what was left of the grampus. The explorers followed their tracks along the beach and deeper into a nearby woods where they discovered a "more sumptuous" graveyard, this one surrounded by a crude wooden fence.

Although this burial ground was grander than those they had previously looted at Corn Hill, "Yet we digged none of them up, but only viewed them and went our way," writes Bradford. Apparently, they belatedly realized that if they wanted to make friends with the local tribes, looting their graves was not the thing to do. Or, perhaps they simply lacked appropriate digging tools.

Bone weary and faint from lack of food—they had eaten nothing all day—they signaled the shallop trailing them offshore to come in for the night. Finding dry firewood in the sudden darkness was difficult but they managed to gather enough to last the night "which cost us a great deal of labor." What little food they still had was warmed over the driftwood fire and gratefully eaten. Each man prepared a bit of open space around the coals, spread his gear and fell into welcome, much needed sleep.

Chapter Twelve

FINDING CAPTAIN MYLES STANDISH

The First Encounter

Their slumbers did not last long. "About midnight we heard a great and hideous howl which caused the sentinel to call out, "Arm, arm." Grabbing nearby muskets, shots were quickly fired into the darkness and the howling ceased. What had it been? One of the sailors said it sounded like wolves he had heard on a previous voyage to Newfoundland. Reassured and still very tired, everyone but the sentinels resumed their interrupted rest.

While it was still quite dark, the explorers began to stir. A few of them stoked the fire with freshly gathered driftwood and began to prepare a bit of breakfast. Worried that their weapons might not function because of the dampness, some of the men decided to test fire them. They did so and, expecting to sail off in a short while, they did not reload. Instead, they took the muskets, along with their personal armor, down to the beach and stowed it all in the beached shallop.

Standish objected to this and cautioned the men that they must always keep muskets loaded and close at hand. But these were strong-willed men whose very religion was based upon rejection of higher earthly authority. Standish had not yet fully established himself in their minds as one able to issue commands to the Saints. This foolish disregard of his expertise and authority nearly cost all of them their lives.

Fortunately, the low tide the previous evening had prevented the shallop from being dragged to higher ground which now meant the muskets could not be stowed without getting wet feet. Not wanting to lug the heavy smooth bores back up the slope, they took the easy choice. Quickly, lest Standish see what they were doing, some of the men wrapped blankets around their muskets, left them on the beach and went up the hill to enjoy a bit of warm breakfast.

17th Century Blunderbuss

The Indians attacked without warning.

But presently, all on the sudden, they heard a great and strange cry, which they knew to be the same voices they heard in the night, though they varied their notes; and one of their company being abroad came running in and cried, "They are men! Indians! Indians!" And withal, their arrows came flying amongst them. (2)

Chapter Twelve

FINDING CAPTAIN MYLES STANDISH

The First Encounter

With daylight impending, there was no time to waste. Once the muskets were discovered, as would certainly happen at first light, they were finished. Standish issued another order, this one unquestioned: those without their weapons would have to make a run for them. "They came running out with coats of mail on and cutlasses in their hands," Bradford recalls.

The Indians tried to cut them off, but fear gave the sprinters added speed. This being the first time any of them had faced an enemy intent upon spilling blood, even those who had lately complained of being unwell fairly flew down the slope. "Our men were no sooner come to their arms, but the enemy was ready to assault them. The cry of our enemies was dreadful."

Flinging the covering blankets aside, the desperate men seized their muskets and swung them about, bluffing. The muskets were still unloaded but it kept the Indians at a respectful distance, shooting arrows from behind trees. Reloading quickly, the colonists put their muskets to good use. "They soon got their arms and let fly amongst them and quickly stopped their violence." The bravery of one Indian especially impressed Bradford:

> Yet there was a lusty man and valiant, who was thought to be their Captain, and stood behind a tree within half a musket shot of us, and there let his arrows fly at us; he stood there for three musket shots until one (Standish) took full aim at him, and made the bark fly about his ears, after which he gave an extraordinary cry and away they went all.

"Afterward, they gave God solemn thanks and praise for their deliverance," writes Bradford. The expedition had been a hairsbreadth away from a massacre. Without their strongest and bravest, the rest of the colony would surely have been wiped out as well. It had lasted a few minutes only, by no means a real battle but the Puritans considered it a significant victory and dignified the little dust-up with a name by which it is still known. The modern Pilgrim driving along the Cape Cod U.S. Highway 6 near the village of North Eastham will see signs showing the way to the site of the "First Encounter."

Shortly after the skirmish with the Indians, the colonists continued exploring the lower Cape. By this time, they had a much clearer idea of what they needed; as Standish had been telling them all along, defensive considerations had to be the number one priority. A decent harbor for shipping was also agreed upon as an absolute must for their little colony. After sailing along the inside Cape Cod shore for nearly forty miles without finding an acceptable harbor and habitation site, it was decided to look for the place earlier recommended to them by Captain John Smith. He had given them a crude map for a harbor they had not yet investigated. It was time for them to leave the inland Cape shore and head across the bay to the continental mainland.

Chapter Twelve

FINDING CAPTAIN MYLES STANDISH

The First Encounter

The sailors assured them that once they changed course and got closer to the mainland lee shore, the seas would be calmer and the sailing much smoother. But it did not happen; instead, the winds grew stronger and gustier. Sailing directly downwind under such circumstances is a tricky business that requires a strong, experienced hand on the tiller to hold the vessel on course and keep it from broaching (turning sideways). Once the pressure of the wind on the sail forces the boat even slightly to port or starboard, it is almost impossible in a strong wind to keep the shallow-draft boat from broaching after which the vessel is liable to swamp and sink.

Masters Mate Clark, unable to handle the tiller by himself, called for assistance; it took two strong men to hold the shallop's stern to the wind. However, rough waves and the bobbing action of the boat caused the heavy rudder to lift off the pintles, a hinge-like device that holds the rudder to the vessel's stern. To the horror of them all, the rudder swung free and promptly disappeared into the depths of the ocean. Masters Mate Clark immediately ordered the oars shipped and manned. It would be up to the oarsmen to keep the boat on course; the entrance to the harbor was just ahead.

Suddenly, without warning, the overstressed mast snapped into three pieces and fell overboard. The sails, still attached, acted as a dragging anchor, pulling the shallop almost to a dead stop, broadside to the waves, each succeeding wave sloshing gallons of water into the boat. Fortunately, the experienced sailors, anticipating just this possibility, were prepared; they fell to with axes, sabers and hatchets, desperately hacking at backstays, shrouds, halyards and sheets. A minute or two more and it would have been all over for them. Once freed, the tangled mess disappeared into the depths of the dark, raging ocean.

Clark guided the oarsmen to pull for a small opening barely visible in the breakers ahead. With the wind pushing them at an unbelievably rapid rate, the crippled shallop shot through the narrow gap into suddenly calm water. Darkness had fallen, and unsure of what was waiting for them ashore, they decided it was safest to remain in the beached shallop until daylight. They soon changed their minds. First one and then another decided to take their chances on dry land, reasoning that they probably had not been seen anyway, it being unlikely that anyone would be lurking about in such weather. In spite of the risk a fire presented, they built one anyway; it was either that or freeze. They gathered driftwood, but the wind and the dampness made it extremely hard to light. After much effort, they got a large fire going and then used more driftwood to create a makeshift windbreak but soon the wind shifted and it became useless. Too cold and tired to build another, they huddled together and waited for daylight. Curiously, Bradford seems to have forgotten just how miserable they had all been. In his memoirs, he notes only that it "froze hard."

Chapter Twelve

FINDING CAPTAIN MYLES STANDISH

The First Encounter

The next morning, a welcome sun allowed the half-frozen men to move about sufficiently to discover that there had been no danger from Indians after all; they had spent the night on a small island, some distance from the mainland shore. In the light of day, they later realized that Clark had taken them through the harbor shoals at the only passage that could have saved them. The grateful survivors named the island, "Clark's Island" in honor of John Clark, who had so miraculously piloted the battered shallop to safety shortly before they were lost at sea in fatal darkness. The little island still bears his name.

Saturday morning, December 10, 1620, the tired and battered men explored the island, thinking it might be a good place to build their town. In the meantime, some of them patched up their shallop for the long row back to the Mayflower.

"In the morning we marched about it and found no inhabitants at all. Here we made our rendezvous all that day, being Saturday." It also being a "fair sun shining day," they dried equipment, rested, and gave thanks for their deliverance.

The next day, Sunday, they honored the Sabbath as usual and stayed on the island. On Monday the weather improved and they explored deeper into the harbor. For the first time, everyone was pleased; the harbor was large and deep enough for even larger ships. They saw several small brooks, convenient for drinking water as well as gentle hills and patches of land already cleared for planting.

This was definitely the place Captain Smith had recommended, and for once, he did not exaggerate. Plimouth Harbor, as they spelled it, pleased Bradford very much: "It is in fashion like a sickle or fishhook and compassed with a goodly land. In the bay are two fine islands, uninhabited, wherein is nothing but wood, oaks, pines, walnut beech, sassafras, vines and other trees which we know not." The farmers among them were delighted with the rich, black soil. They found native cherry and plum trees along with evidence of warm weather plants such as watercress, leeks, onions and other herbs. It looked like a wonderful site indeed.

> . . . a most hopeful place with innumerable store of excellent good fowl, and there cannot but be fish in their seasons. Skate, cod, turbot, and herring we have tasted of. There is also abundance of mussels, the greatest and best that ever we saw, and crabs and lobsters in their time infinite . . . the best water we have ever drunk is here. (3)

Chapter Twelve

FINDING CAPTAIN MYLES STANDISH

The First Encounter

With no mast and no rudder, the explorers had a long row across the bay back to the tip of Cape Cod to reach the anchorage of the Mayflower. Their expedition was supposed to be a brief one and they had been gone an entire week, but they were sure they would be forgiven; the news they were bringing to the ship was what everyone had been hoping for. Instead, they were greeted with the worst news imaginable. William Bradford's wife, Dorothy May, had fallen overboard and drowned.

We can only imagine how shocking this news must have been to Bradford, but strangely, when he compiled his "History of Plimouth Plantation" twenty years later, he hardly mentions it. Under the heading of "Deaths," he writes only, "Dorothy May, wife of William Bradford."

Because of this abruptness, some historians speculate that she committed suicide, an act believed by the Puritans to be an unforgivable sin. Others argue that Dorothy May would never have taken her life because the Bradford's had left a young son back in England, probably under the care of Pastor John Robinson, and would send for him when conditions in the colony permitted.

On the other hand, poor Dorothy had reasons to be depressed; for the past four months, she had been living under extremely stressful conditions and she knew it would get even worse as soon as they moved ashore. Further, many of her shipboard friends had died of the General Sickness and others were lying sick in increasing numbers. Also, it may be that, aware of the bad weather and the unexpected length of time the explorers were gone, she had become convinced that her husband was not ever coming back to her.

Chapter Thirteen

FINDING CAPTAIN MYLES STANDISH

Moving Ashore

Going Ashore at Provincetown   **from a painting by Mike Haywood**

Master Jones ordered the Mayflower's anchor hoisted on the 15th of December. Most of the passengers had not participated in the various shore expeditions and were extremely glad to see the Provincetown Bay disappear astern. They had been stuck aboard for five long weeks after spending two full months crossing the Atlantic. Although they had been allowed to go ashore briefly several times, they were sick to death of shipboard living.

Jones intended to take the Mayflower directly across the bay to Plymouth Harbor, which under normal conditions, would have been a comfortable two-hour sail at most. However, because the beamy old Mayflower was unable to sail close to the wind, and the breeze being contrary, it took several long reaches to get to the harbor entrance. Jones had never been there before, and being a cautious shipmaster, the low tide and following winds caused him to be leery of taking the Mayflower past the outer shoals and sand bars into the harbor.

Chapter Thirteen

FINDING CAPTAIN MYLES STANDISH

Moving Ashore

Jones was being prudent; if he put his ship on the rocks, there was no possibility of rescue. He ordered the helmsman to bring the ship about and they returned to their original anchorage. His passengers were very unhappy; some even wondered aloud if they would ever again set foot upon dry land. As it turned out, they had not long to wait. "But it pleased God that . . . the wind came fair, and we put to sea again and came safely into a safe harbor." Even then, it was a near thing. "Within half an hour the wind changed, so that if we had been lingered but a little, we had gone back to Cape Cod." (2)

The Mayflower arrived at Plimouth Harbor on December 16, 1620. While the Puritans spent the day praying and giving thanks for their deliverance, Standish, never a member of their congregation, recruited some of the other "strangers" to help him prepare to off-load his precious cannon, powder and associated military equipment.

For security reasons perhaps, women were not included in the first landing party, but they came ashore soon after. The exact spot where they stepped ashore is unknown, but clearly it was not the Plymouth Rock site as now commonly believed. This American fable came to life many years after the actual event. It began like this: In the early 1800's, nearly two hundred years after the Mayflower anchored at Plimouth Harbor, Deacon Spooner, an elderly Plymouth storyteller, claimed that when he was a youngster some old man of his acquaintance told him that, when he himself had been a boy, his father had informed him that a certain Plimouth beach rock was the spot where the Pilgrims first stepped ashore. There has never been any other confirmation of this convoluted tale but the folks at the Plymouth Chamber of Commerce find it quite convincing.

The colonists organized themselves into nineteen "families" with the older, unattached boys and servants put under the close supervision of older and presumably wiser, married men. Everyone agreed that a "common house" would be built first, followed by dwellings for individual families. It took a full week before they began the actual construction of the common house. A lot of preliminary work had to be done.

Another reason for the delay was the time wasted looking for two men who became lost while gathering thatching material for the roof. "This day (12 January 1621), two of our people put us in great sorrow and care." A crew of four went down to the marsh to cut reed thatch and two of them, John Goodman and Peter Browne, went farther afield searching for fresh materials, leaving the other two to bind up what had already been cut. When the two men did not return by dark, it was assumed that the Indians had killed or captured them. "The next day, work stopped wile an armed search party ranged for miles looking for them without success which much discomforted us all," according to Bradford.

Chapter Thirteen

FINDING CAPTAIN MYLES STANDISH

Moving Ashore

The missing men's two dogs had caused the problem; they had jumped a deer and chased it with Brown and Goodman following, trying to call them back. With no sun to orient them and in unfamiliar territory without a compass, they became lost, wandering from hill to knoll all afternoon, shouting for help. As the day waned, it turned cold with rain and then snow.

Bradford recalls that everyone was very concerned because "They were slenderly appareled and had neither victuals nor any weapons but each one his sickle. They ranged about but could find no shelter and were forced to make the earth their bed and the element their covering. During the long night, they thought they heard the roaring of lions."

Whatever it actually was—a lynx perhaps—it may have saved them from sinking into slumber and death by freezing. The same large mastiff bitch that led them astray probably kept them alive by keeping them awake. She wanted to go after the "lion," forcing the men to hold on to her by the scruff of her neck, so they walked up and down under the tree all night, an extremely cold night.

The lost men considered climbing a tree to "escape the lions, but as that would prove an intolerably cold lodging, they stood at the tree's root so that when the lions came they might take their opportunity of climbing up." (7, 14)

The next morning the two men climbed a hill and were able to see the ocean in the distance. They set off, becoming lost many more times during the day. Finally, in near dark, they stumbled back to the plantation ". . . ready to faint with travel and want of victuals, and almost famished with cold." Goodman's feet were so badly swollen from frostbite that his precious shoes had to be cut from his feet. They never did see any lions.

As ever, there still were differing opinions as to the exact location of their communal site. Some wanted to be closer to the already-cleared fields; others thought it important to be adjacent to the forest for convenient access to firewood and timber. All of them wanted easy access to fresh water. A few dissidents even said they disapproved of the Plimouth site; they preferred the Cape itself. For three more precious days they debated the pros and the cons, finally deciding on the Plimouth mainland. "We could not now take time for further search or consideration, our victuals being much spent, especially our beare." (2)

At the proper time, Standish weighed in with his priorities. He reminded them that elsewhere in New England Indians had wiped out entire settlements. Better than anyone, he appreciated just how close the recent encounter with hostile savages had been and how easily it could have led to this colony being the next to go.

Chapter Thirteen

FINDING CAPTAIN MYLES STANDISH

Moving Ashore

A military man would have argued that defensive considerations outweighed all others; visibility and good fields of fire for musket and cannon were crucial to their survival. Having been so recently under attack, they accepted his advice and went a step further: along with a common house, their first building priority would be putting up some defensive fortifications.

For his fort, Captain Standish chose a site on a long, gentle slope that led down to the bay, a natural elevation where he could mount cannon as soon as they could be brought ashore. It was not convenient to the brook and its fresh water, but this was offset by it being far enough away from the woods so that Indians could not catch them unawares.

Following more debate, they staked out the dimensions of the palisade and a proper fort that would come later, laid out the individual house lots and the main street that would run through the town center. Others went into the woods to select and begin cutting and shaping logs needed for the construction of the outer palisade.

The house walls were of the familiar wattle and daub construction with each building corner made of mud brick or logs set into deep holes in the ground. Several coats of clay and mud were daubed into the interlaced wattles of sticks and allowed to dry. It was important to have the roof in place and thatched before this step occurred or it could all be washed away in a single rainstorm.

Wattle and daub detail

Chapter Thirteen

FINDING CAPTAIN MYLES STANDISH

Moving Ashore

Back in England, none of them had ever lived in luxury; they had been simple country folk used to Elizabethan-style yeoman cottages, one or two-rooms only. Now they built the same familiar structures they were used to; lattice-woven sticks daubed with New England clay. Also as in old England, the new dwellings were usually chimneyless; the smoke was meant to simply drift upward and escape through a small opening in the peak of the roof thatching. The smoky lofts served as a good place to hang meat if they had any to put there. They were accustomed to using wheat straw for thatching but, there being none available, cattail reeds from nearby marshes were substituted. They would have much preferred the straw, it being lighter and much easier to work.

Roof thatching detail

The year 1620 closed cold and rainy. There was precious little for them to celebrate; people were dying in alarming numbers, but at least the frame of the common house was finished. They were immensely pleased to have finally accomplished something constructive; the colonists moved into their first shelter on the 14th of January. But, their satisfaction was short lived, ending abruptly when an errant spark from a stove inside the common house set the roof afire.

Chapter Thirteen

FINDING CAPTAIN MYLES STANDISH

Moving Ashore

The fire could not have happened at a worse time; they had just off loaded their powder supply and it was stored within. They were able to save the powder and mud walls but the thatched roof was a total loss. Had it reached the powder, it could have been a lot more serious.

But the camaraderie did not last; as soon as the first houses were about to be finished, serious bickering began. Those who had been doing most of the work wanted their families to be first to move into the completed dwellings. Others said it was not their fault they were too sick to work and that it should be done by lot or seniority. A meeting was called: "We agreed that every man should build his own house, thinking that by this course men would make more haste than working in common." Thus ended the first attempt at communistic endeavor in the North American continent.

Once again, John Goodman was frightened by a wild animal. Suffering from his frostbitten feet and unable to help with the work, he decided to take a therapeutic walk with his spaniel. The frolicking dog ran into a pair of wolves, and with the wolves in hot pursuit, fled back to Goodman, diving for cover between his legs. Goodman claimed he fought the wolves off with a stick after which he says they sat on their tails "grinning a good while" before going on about their business. This is how Goodman tells it, but then, he is the same one who heard the lions. How his frostbitten feet allowed him to walk in the woods, but prevented him from helping with the shelter building is unclear.

The good weather continued for ten more blessed days. Some of the ailing Pilgrims were able to help a bit. The common-house roof was re-thatched and a small storage shed was completed, after which it was stocked with Standish's gunpowder, along with other supplies brought ashore from the Mayflower.

Master Jones noted several Indians watching the construction from nearby Clarke Island, where the explorers had once spent such a miserable night. In spite of the colonists' attempts to signal their good will toward them, the Indians kept their distance. Their intentions were becoming increasingly worrisome; friendly relations were vital to the colony's trading success and they had yet to make contact with any of them except on a warlike basis. Their lurking silence was beginning to look increasingly ominous and was a subject of many discussions amongst the nervous colonists.

February brought with it ever increasing, strong, cold, winds; often with driving rain and sleet, the worst yet. The recently daubed mud walls began to wash away; with little chance to dry properly. It was not long before the only thing holding out the cold winds was a bare, open latticework of sticks, keeping them all in a constant, cold misery.

Chapter Thirteen

FINDING CAPTAIN MYLES STANDISH

Moving Ashore

Now that most of its cargo was removed, the Mayflower at anchor rode much higher in the water, allowing wind and waves to drag its anchor. It was in danger of being beached or destroyed on the rocks, so in spite of the rough seas, the sailors climbed into open boats to tow the wayward vessel into deeper water.

Master Jones became a hero when he shot five more geese while going ashore from his ship. At the same time, his musket shots frightened away several Indians who had killed a deer nearby. It was a special bonanza for Jones and his men when they donated the carcass to the Plantation, where it was promptly cut up, cooked and served to the delight of everyone. Encouraged by Jones's success, one of the Pilgrims went goose hunting and while hiding in the reeds, saw what appeared to be an Indian war party moving stealthily towards the plantation. As soon as he dared, the hunter dashed back to spread the alarm.

Standish and Francis Cook were cutting wood nearby. Upon hearing the shouts, they dropped their tools and dashed home to prepare for the expected attack. No Indians appeared, but they stayed on full alert until dark, eventually seeing a large fire near the place where the Indians had been. The next morning, February 17th, when Standish and Cook went back to recover their implements, they were chagrined to find them missing. Perhaps the Indians considered it as compensation for the missing corn.

Although it had been a false alarm, the colonists could not risk being caught unawares like this again. Under Standish's direction, security measures were redoubled. Closer attention was paid to weapons and training in their use. Since dampness tended to make powder unreliable, Captain Standish ordered that henceforth, all muskets were to be carefully recharged and re-primed daily.

Another conference was called and it was agreed that it was time to give their military officer the rank and authority he needed to provide for the defense of the colony. In spite of the obviousness of this decision, this authority had been previously withheld; even now it took a good fright to get them all to do it. "We chose Myles Standish our Captain and gave him command in affairs." This long overdue action, not taken until two months after they arrived in New England, again demonstrates the Puritan's reluctance to acknowledge higher authority, even when it was clearly in their best interest to do so; it had taken the threat of an attack to convince them.

Chapter Fourteen

FINDING CAPTAIN MYLES STANDISH

The General Sickness

Secret night burial

> Being the depth of winter, and wanting houses and other comforts; being infected with the scurvy and other diseases, which this long voiage and the inacomodate condition had brought upon them; so as there dyed some times 2 or 3 of a day. (2)

The "General Sickness," as they called it, continued to spread; six died of it in December, eight more in January. By the end of February, seventeen more were gone. The deaths in the month of March continued unabated; thirteen more succumbed. Almost half of their original number were now gone, all of them much loved spouses, children, dear friends.

It was obvious that the natives were keeping close watch on the daily activities of the colonists. Fearful that the Indians would take advantage of their dire situation, they buried their dead in secret, careful to do so only on moonless nights, always camouflaging the graves. It is unclear how many dwellings were completed by this time but most of the colonists were living ashore. The sick and dying were kept out of sight, cautioned to be quiet lest they give way to themselves and expose the colony's desperate situation to unsympathetic tribesmen, many of them who would be not at all sorry, perhaps even pleased, to have all of them gone.

Chapter Fourteen

FINDING CAPTAIN MYLES STANDISH

The General Sickness

In his "History of Plimouth Colony," Bedford describes the quiet heroism of their military leader, presenting a side of Myles Standish that few historians ever acknowledge. Bradford relates that very few of the colonists did not get sick: ". . . of these were William Brewster . . . and Myles Standish, Captain and military commander, unto whom my selfe, and many others, were much beholden in our low and sicke condition." Bradford continues:

> . . .to their great comendations be it spoken, they spared no pains, night or day, but with abundance of toyle and hazard of their owne health, fetched woode, made fires, drest meat, made beds, washed their lothsome cloaths, cloathed and uncloathed them; in a word, did all the homly and necessarie offices for them which dainty and quesie stomacks cannot endure to hear named; and all this willingly and cherfully, without any grudging in the least, shewing herein their true love unto there freinds and bretheren. A rare example and worthy to be remembered. (2)

In stark contrast, Master Christopher Jones and his Mayflower crews remained safely (as they thought) aboard ship, and were not at all helpful to those on shore.

> To conserve the ship's beer for themselves, sailors hurried the passengers ashore where they could drink brook water. When one of the dying Pilgrims on shore sent a message to the ship asking for beer . . .it was answered that "if he were their own father he should have none." (2)

The situation quickly changed when the ship's company became afflicted. One by one, the officers and sailors sickened and most of them soon died. First to be struck down was the ship's cook; he was quickly followed by the bosun, three quartermasters, the gunner and finally, Master Jones himself.

Due to Christian kindness or perhaps simple pragmatism—they all knew that if Master Jones died, there was no one qualified to replace him—those able to row a boat took him ashore and he was nursed along with the rest. There was little any one could do for him, but it must have cheered him anyway; obviously, his crewmembers could not have cared less.

Chapter Fourteen

FINDING CAPTAIN MYLES STANDISH

The General Sickness

After a bit, their forgiving kindness—or his own thirst—caused Jones to suffer a change of heart regarding his precious beare. He sent a message to the ship, ordering them to bring ashore a goodly supply, ". . . for beare for them that had need of it, even though we drink water homeward bound." The sick sailors still aboard the Mayflower utterly failed to help one another: ". . . (they) let one another to lie and die like dogs," as one of them later said.

Few escaped the sickness, Saints or Strangers. Along with tending the sick and burying the dead, those still able to function had huts to build; there was no one else. Of the twenty-one Puritan men and six boys, seldom were more than half a dozen fit for duty at any one time. Before the month ended, the Colony Governor, John Carver, also succumbed. Although William Bradford had been quite ill, he was beginning to recuperate, and though far from well, was elected to take Carver's place.

Despite his constant and tender care, Myles' wife, Rose was one of seven who died in January. Almost nothing is known about his beloved "English Rose." The children, especially the girls, generally fared better than did the adults, probably because of the better food they received due to parental sacrifice. Of the eleven girls that boarded the Mayflower, ten survived. Of the twenty-one boys, a number of them indentured orphans, there were just fifteen who made it through the first winter.

By the 1st of April, only fifty-six Saints and Strangers were still alive, some barely so and the dying was far from over. Six months from now there would only be twenty-three of the original adults still living. One who did not make it was Susanna White's husband William. He died soon after she gave birth to a son they named Peregrine. A woman alone, especially one with an infant, could not afford to spend much time grieving. She agreed to marry Edward Winslow a few weeks later, his wife having died shortly before. Winslow was fortunate to find a helpmeet. Of the fourteen wives boarding the Mayflower back in England, just four were still alive. Only two of the emigrating couples would survive as partners; Mary and William Brewster and Elizabeth and Stephen Hopkins. Among those losing spouses were William Bradford, Edward Winslow, Gilbert Winslow, Isaac Allerton, Samuel Fuller and Myles Standish.

Had they arrived in New England properly prepared for fishing, they could have lived off the ocean's bounty alone. Too proud, ignorant, or too arrogant to seek expert counsel when they still had the opportunity back in England, they supplied themselves with fishhooks too large and fishing nets that were too small. They would suffer terribly for such abysmal planning. John Carver had acted as their agent in England and was probably the person most responsible for dealing with the chandlers. But, he was apparently not blamed for the poor planning and lack of proper equipment since they elected him to two terms as colony governor before he died.

Chapter Fourteen

FINDING CAPTAIN MYLES STANDISH

The General Sickness

The New England sun rose a bit earlier each day, traversing an ever-higher arc in the mostly clear blue sky. The snow began to melt, and gradually, the ice left the ponds, encouraging the geese to come within range of the musketeers. At last, the earth warmed sufficiently for them to begin working the soil. "We digged our ground and sowed our garden seeds." Peas were probably the first, followed by greens such as lettuce, these being best able to tolerate chilly nights and the occasional late snowfall.

The terrible sickness apparently had run its course, and though many recuperating colonists were still unable to help much with the house building, there were now a lot fewer houses needed with so many of them no longer among the living

Chapter Fifteen

FINDING CAPTAIN MYLES STANDISH

Pilgrim Hall, Duxbury

Pilgrim Hall, Duxbury

For an entire year before we began our genealogic excursion, Elaine Corbett, volunteer researcher at the Pilgrim Hall in Duxbury, and I had exchanged letters concerning Standish research. We also traded bits of information about our families and ourselves, eventually agreeing that Ruth and I would come to Duxbury so we could meet in person. We would go to the Pilgrim Hall Museum and see all the other points of interest which, Elaine assured us, were well worth a visit.

It had not taken much urging, once Elaine told us about Duxbury's fabulous Fourth of July parade and described how spectacular fireworks would arch high over a replica of the old Mayflower as it sat anchored in Plymouth Bay just offshore. We immediately began making travel plans. This trip would be more than just an opportunity to visit the site of the Pilgrim's

Chapter Fifteen

FINDING CAPTAIN MYLES STANDISH

Pilgrim Hall, Duxbury

landing and walk the ground where they had struggled so valiantly to survive in the new world; it would give us a chance to do some first-hand research on our way there and back. Elaine had reminded me of the often-repeated adage that our ancestors tend to wait for just the right person to come along and discover them.

We had already noted that the Standish progeny were far less numerous than those of the John Aldens. Barbara and Myles had seven children, but only two of them had children of their own. It seemed to us that it ought to be fairly easy to track down each Standish line, since there were only about two dozen adult Standishes living at the beginning of the early-to-mid 1800's, the period when our Young ancestor, John, would have married Amy Standish.

Alexander, the eldest Standish son, married Sarah, daughter of Priscilla and John Alden. Obviously, the poet Longfellow had it all wrong. His famous poem "The Courtship of Myles Standish" depicted Myles as a bitter, rejected suitor ("Why don't you speak for yourself, John?"). According to Longfellow, Myles held a long-time grudge at his rejection in favor of John Alden. But this did not square with the fact that the Alden and Standish families were life-long friends. As we soon discovered for ourselves, so were many of their descendants for at least the next one hundred and seventy-five years.

Back in Elkhart, Cousin Walter Young had been quite certain that Amy Standish Young had been born in Ashfield, but had no documentation to prove that this was so. When I obtained a copy of Ashfield Vital Records, it did not list her as Israel's daughter, although his other four children were listed, indicating that she was born somewhere else, if not to someone else; but where and to whom?

Mansfield, Connecticut, Israel's birthplace, had at first seemed a good possibility. On our way to Plymouth, we had stopped at the Mansfield Historical Society to see if Amy's birth was recorded there, but it was not. Israel had been born there in 1738, but his father, Miles, had pulled up stakes and moved his family to Ashfield when Israel was still an infant.

As it turned out, less than a week later I was able to supply the Mayflower Society with—and they accepted—the names and birth dates of all the 5th generation Israel Standish children, including the missing Amie, as she herself spelled it, and another sibling named Submit, whose birth was also previously unrecorded. As will be seen, this breakthrough was due to the kind assistance of the staff of the neighboring Franklin County Register of Deeds, plus a lot of dumb luck—more about that later.

Chapter Fifteen

FINDING CAPTAIN MYLES STANDISH

Pilgrim Hall, Duxbury

We arrived in charming Duxbury at high noon on the 4th of July, 1990. We were anxious to meet our resident Standish expert, see the famous Standish Monument, visit the re-created Plymouth Colony and immerse ourselves in Standish history and memorabilia at the Pilgrim Society Museum, established in 1824 and the oldest continuously operating museum in America.

Families were already busy positioning themselves along the parade route as we drove along Duxbury's winding streets to our bed & breakfast inn. At our request, Elaine had reserved a very nice place for us to stay, one of the few such B & B's in Duxbury, conveniently located just a short walk from the old John Alden home, which we later visited. Elaine resided in Duxbury and when I first wrote to the Plymouth Mayflower Society for information about Myles Standish, I was referred by them to the Pilgrim Museum in nearby Duxbury; just the advice I most needed.

Duxbury was founded in 1637, when Myles Standish and his good friend, John Alden, removed themselves a comfortable distance away from the daily goings on at Plimouth Plantation. Although Duxbury is only seven miles or so from modern-day Plymouth by the Shore road, it is less than half the distance by sail. Considering the holiday traffic we experienced getting from one site to the other, sailing would have been a lot quicker.

For a modest fee, I had enrolled as a Duxbury Hall Society Associate, entitling me to assistance from volunteer researchers. I had requested Elaine Corbet, after being informed that she was well versed in Standish lineage. She had supplied me with much helpful information, so Ruth and I were keenly looking forward to meeting her in person. We found her to be charming and delightful—fun to be with. Her husband, Jim, joined us and the four of us got acquainted while strolling the mile or so to a convenient site from which we could get a good view of the parade and the harbor beyond. The 4th of July in Duxbury is a major civic celebration; there were scores of marching units from all over the state. I would not have believed there were so many fire engines with such loud sirens in all of Massachusetts.

The weather was ideal. The spacious lawn leading down to the waterfront area began filling with thousands of tourists and local citizens gathering to watch the fireworks. Brightly colored blankets were spread on the grassy slope, alive with excited children running everywhere, anxious for darkness to fall and the fireworks to begin. Suddenly, spectacular rockets arched high over and beyond the Mayflower II, lasting for an hour or more. In the midst of the whirling star clusters and screaming rockets it amused me to speculate—what would the inhabitants of the old Plimouth Plantation have thought of all this joyility? Or the Indians?

Chapter Fifteen

FINDING CAPTAIN MYLES STANDISH

Pilgrim Hall, Duxbury

When the fireworks were over, Jim and Elaine escorted us a short distance to a wharfside restaurant, where by Elaine's thoughtful prearrangement, we were seated on a second-floor balcony directly facing the Mayflower II, just a short distance away. Without a doubt, it was the finest seafood we had ever tasted. The strait-laced Puritans would not have approved of so much joyility, but for Ruth and me, it was the perfect finale to a perfect day.

Mayflower II

The next morning Elaine met us on the steps of the venerable old Pilgrim Hall, an imposing structure built in 1884, proud to be the oldest continuously operating museum in America and still the social and cultural center of Duxbury; (it has since been remodeled and enlarged).

We were warmly welcomed by the curator, Ellen Driver. She was aware of the purpose of our visit and was obviously pleased to take us directly to the Myles Standish room. Almost immediately, my eyes fell upon what appeared to be a young lad's sword hanging on the far wall.

Chapter Fifteen

FINDING CAPTAIN MYLES STANDISH

Pilgrim Hall, Duxbury

Next, I noticed a small chair placed near a lighted Plexiglas display case. The chair was obviously a sturdy one but much too small for an adult, or so I first thought. But I should have known better; I had momentarily forgotten that I was there to view the personal artifacts of Captain Myles Standish, a man well known for his small size.

A closer look at the Standish sword made it obvious that this was not a child's toy; it was made of sturdy, well-tempered steel with a hand guard designed to deflect a serious blow from another slicing blade. But still, it was hard not to smile at the thought of the diminutive captain in full armor, sword in hand, challenging a bunch of Indians ready to do him and his men serious harm.

Then I recalled that I was not the first person to underestimate the Captain. An Indian named Wituwamat paid with his life for making essentially the same misjudgment and sneering at the angry little red-faced man standing before him.

Back in England, Pastor Robinson was not pleased when he heard about Wituwamat's untimely demise. "O would that you had converted some before you killed any," he is supposed to have said. Myles Standish remains a testament to what we all sometimes forget; it is not the size, it is the situation and the spirit.

The Standish chair had the same effect upon my Ruth. Although much sturdier, it was proportioned quite the same as a prized heirloom that came to America with her great-grandmother, Mary Kelly of the Emerald Isles. Mary was a bit less than five feet tall and her custom-made rocking chair often has the same effect upon our guests when they first see it. "Is it a real, rocking chair," they often ask.

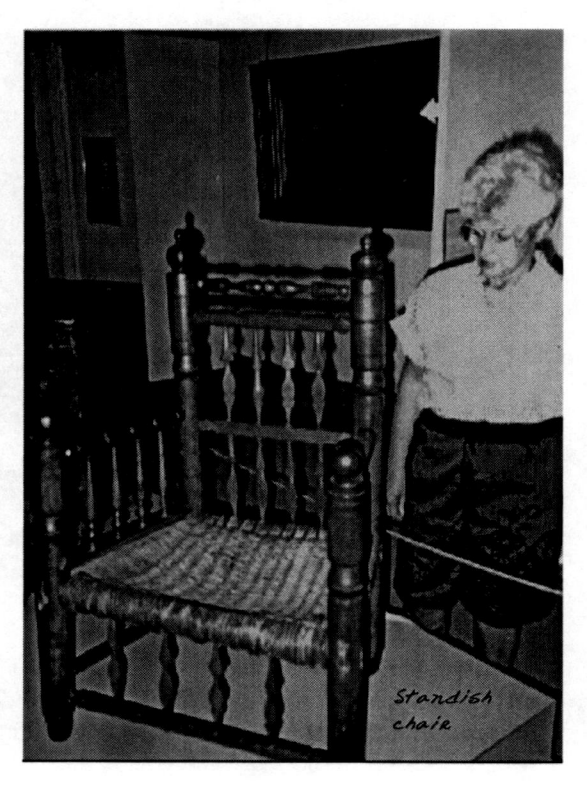

Ruth admires Myles' favorite chair

Chapter Fifteen

FINDING CAPTAIN MYLES STANDISH

Pilgrim Hall, Duxbury

Of the many other Standish artifacts in the room, one of the most interesting was an ordinary-sized silver cup, highlighted under an overhead spotlight and protected inside a small Plexiglas showcase, leaving no doubt that this was an important Standish possession. Curator Driver left the room and came back with a small screwdriver which she used to remove the securing screws after which she removed the protective casing. She had me don a pair of white cotton gloves and ceremoniously handed me the cup.

"Turn it over," she said. There, etched on the bottom was the name "John Robinson." He was the Scrooby Congregation pastor who remained behind to act as their agent. Standish family tradition claims that the cup was a gift of friendship from Robinson to Standish. While this cannot be proven, it is known that the cup was made around 1610, but heavily reworked by a silversmith in the 1720s. In any case, it is known as the Robinson cup and it was a thrill for me to hold. I briefly considered asking that it be filled with Pilgrim beare, but wisely thought better of it.

The Robinson – Standish friendship cup

Chapter Sixteen

FINDING CAPTAIN MYLES STANDISH

Plimouth Plantation

A modeled overview of Plimouth Plantation, c. 1627

Entering the re-created Plimouth village is much like discovering a marvelous time machine; one minute you are standing outside the palisade walls and a few steps later, you suddenly find yourself transported to a 1620's colonist settlement in the midst of the Wampanoag nation. One cannot help being drawn into plantation activities as it was lived some seven years after the Mayflower landing. Continue walking and you notice neat rows of timber-framed houses (the wattle and daub construction had to be replaced with more permanent sawn lumber). However, the buildings still have reed-thatched roofs, some of them undergoing repair. Step inside any one of them to witness women and girls going about every day household chores, all of them authentically garbed and speaking as the colonists did at the time.

Chapter Sixteen

FINDING CAPTAIN MYLES STANDISH

Plimouth Plantation

If one stands quietly by on a hard-packed dirt floor you can watch the busy women vigorously kneading bread dough, stirring a soup kettle suspended over a rough stone fireplace or simply listen to them visit with each other. You do not have to remain silent; ask them a question and they will respond appropriately. But should you cleverly attempt to trip them up by asking if they wished for a gas or electric oven, they will say nothing except perhaps ask you, "Pray sir, what might that be?"

A thatched roof under repair

One fellow was observed perched precariously on rude scaffolding made of spindly tree branches and we stopped to see what he was doing. He had several bundles of freshly cut cattail stems lying on the thatched roof beside him and was in the process of repairing the roof. After removing the rotted thatching, the roofer slid handfuls of freshly cut, three-foot stems under neighboring reeds and then tamped the stem ends into place with a wooden mallet. I was curious to know if he actually went into the marshes to cut the cattails, but he either didn't hear me or was too busy to answer unimportant questions.

Chapter Sixteen

FINDING CAPTAIN MYLES STANDISH

Plimouth Plantation

Plimouth Plantation looking seaward

There was a lot to see. We walked past a small cluster of goats munching purloined vegetables and better understood the need for all those picket fences. We continued on up the hill to the Colony meeting-house and examined the fortifications Standish had so carefully designed. He had positioned his cannon where they commanded excellent fields of fire over the near terrain and the harbor beyond. His musketeers would have played havoc with an enemy attempting to scale the palisade walls. Nearby were a very interesting Wampanoag campsite and dwellings. Our impression of Plimouth Plantation was extremely favorable and highly recommended to anyone with an appreciation of early American history.

(Photos in this chapter are from the Plimouth Plantation Web site)

Chapter Seventeen

FINDING CAPTAIN MYLES STANDISH

Samoset and Squanto

Welcome, Englishmen!

The sun gradually arced ever higher into the zodiac and each successive day lengthened ever so slightly. Bradford recalls March 7th as a cool day with a faint hint of spring that encouraged thoughts of improving their meager, boring diet with a meal of tasty fresh fish: "Master Carver with five others went to the great ponds, which seem to be excellent fishing places." On the way, they saw evidence of deer activity. "Amongst other fowl, they saw one milk white fowl with a very black head." They were all cheered by the sight of what had to be a trumpeter swan, a magnificent early sign of New England spring.

Master Jones, an expert marksman, "brought with him a very fat goose to eat with us, and we had a fat crane and a mallard and a dried tongue. And so we were kindly and friendly together." The ship's beare may have helped.

The 16th of March seemed like a good time to have another meeting. Standish probably wanted to organize his defenders into units he could better control. He needed trusty lieutenants to carry out his orders but this was a democratic army, and probably contrary to Standish's preference, the Puritan elders insisted upon elections for the officers serving under him. The Captain managed to get the rest of his military organization plans approved by the Elders. Even though he was very sick at the time, John Carver was re-elected to a second term as Colony Governor, a term he would barely live long enough to even begin. (*)

Chapter Seventeen

FINDING CAPTAIN MYLES STANDISH

Samoset and Squanto

The red men apparently had an extremely effective intelligence network. Barely an hour after their meeting began, they were interrupted: ". . . on the top of the hill over against us two or three savages presented themselves and made semblance of daring us, as we thought." (2, 14)

> As we were in consultation . . . two savages presented themselves upon the top of a hill about a quarter of a mile or less away from our plantation and made signs unto us to come unto them. (3)

"No, thank you," signaled the colonists: "You come over here." To break the impasse, Standish and Stephen Hopkins met them halfway. As a sign of his peaceful intentions, Standish placed his musket on the ground. Still unconvinced, the Indians drew back into the woods and the parley attempt ended in suspicion and failure.

Standish prepared his men for the battle he now expected. "This caused us to plant our ordinances in places most convenient." With much effort, they hauled four heavy cannon up the long plantation slope, mounted them on wooden platforms and then loaded them for action. Standish's arsenal contained four of the most fearsome weapons on the continent, a Saker, a Minion and two Bases. If the Indians could be intimidated by the sound of musket fire, the roar of these cannon would surely scare them out of their wits, along with any plans they might have to do them mischief.

The Base was a four-and-a-half foot long heavy iron tube with an inch-and-a-half bore. Swivel mounted on a massive wooden pedestal, it could blast a deadly spray of solid lead balls or iron shards. Artillerymen affectionately called it the "Murderer" because of its deadly effect at short-range.

The largest cannon was a Minion. Weighing a full half-ton, it lobbed a three-and-a-half pound ball three-fourths of a mile. The Saker weighed much less, but could fire a two-and-a-half pound ball almost as far as the minion, but hitting anything at that range was more luck than skill. The Minion and the Saker may have been borrowed from the Mayflower arsenal but, she being a wine-transporting merchantman, this seems unlikely. Standish probably acquired them back in Leyden from ordinance left behind when the English army returned home after the late war with the Spanish.

Then, when they least expected it, a full three months after they arrived in New England, and after repeated unsuccessful attempts to establish contact with their neighboring native tribesmen, their luck suddenly changed for the better. Their next colony meeting was interrupted by what appeared to be the very threat they were gathered to discuss.

Chapter Seventeen

FINDING CAPTAIN MYLES STANDISH

Samoset and Squanto

With uncanny timing, a large Indian brave came out of the forest and strode directly to where they sat, causing them no little consternation. "He came boldly all alone among the houses and straight toward the community rendezvous. We intercepted him there, not suffering him to go in, as undoubtedly he would have done out of his boldness."

There were many very sick people lying in a number of dwellings, all of them warned not to make any sounds that would provide the natives with a clue that they were in such desperate straits. Then, to their utter astonishment, the unexpected visitor greeted them with a hearty, "'Welcome, Englishmen!"

The Indian in their midst was an impressive specimen in his early thirties who stood tall and straight. He was "stark naked except for a leather loincloth about his waist with a fringe about a span long or a little more," recalls Bradford. Several shocked Puritans, using the chilly wind for an excuse, "cast a horseman's coat about him."

His name, he informed them in broken, barely understandable English, was Samoset of the Pemaquid Tribe farther up the Maine coast, and that he learned English from an earlier, unsuccessful group of colonists who had attempted to establish themselves on Monhegan Island, (Sir Ferdinando Gorges' Northern Virginia Company).

Samoset told his fascinated audience that he had learned to speak their language from fishermen who had been coming for years to the shore where he lived, a five days journey to the north. The colonists finally learned why there were so few Indians nearby and such conveniently cleared fields. Samoset told them that some four years earlier, a terrible plague wiped out entire tribes. For the Puritans who had been concerned about possible disputes regarding ownership of the land they had appropriated, this was welcome news indeed.

Bradford noted: "There is neither man, woman, nor child remaining, so that there is none to hinder our possession or to lay claim unto it." However, Bradford's assumption was soon proved to be incorrect; there actually was someone left alive with a legitimate claim to the lands they occupied.

A few days later, they would learn that Samoset's friend had been a member of the Patuxet Tribe and it was their cleared lands that the Pilgrims had taken for their own. Bradford makes no further mention of providing restitution.

The colonists may have gotten by with this because, until the arrival of the white men, the idea of land ownership was a foreign concept to the Indian mind. They fought wars over tribal hunting and fishing sites, but land ownership as we know it did not exist for them.

Chapter Seventeen

FINDING CAPTAIN MYLES STANDISH

Samoset and Squanto

Samoset's earlier contact with English sailors left him with a liking for English ale and he asked if he could have some. Their beer supply being rather limited, they gave him instead "stronge water and biscuit and butter and cheese and pudding and a piece of mallard."

After three long months, they had almost given up hope of ever making contact with friendly natives. Now the would-be traders discovered a facet of Indian behavior that would prove troublesome in the months to come; once they came to visit, they overstayed. "All the afternoon we spent in communication with him. We would gladly have been rid of him at night, but he was not willing to go."

Stuck with him but unwilling to offend him, they decided it would be prudent to take Samoset aboard the Mayflower where armed sailors could better watch him. He was willing but the wind was up and the tide was too low to launch the shallop. After quiet but hasty consultation, they escorted him to the home of Stephen Hopkins. Full of good food and strong water, Samoset doubtlessly enjoyed a much better night's rest than did his wary, wakeful host.

They got rid of Samoset the next morning by giving him a ring, a bracelet and a knife. He said he would return soon with a friend named Squanto who spoke much better English. He also told them he would bring along some tribesmen who had beaver skins to trade. The colonists were extremely pleased at this, fur trade being the main reason why they had come to New England. They outfitted Samoset in white man's attire and sent him off to find out when his brethren would bring them the promised furs. He must have been a sight to behold in a high black, Puritan hat, stockings and leather shoes. However, he still thought it insufficient and asked for more adornment. As a final touch, a bright sash was tied around his waist.

Before leaving, Samoset told them yet another reason why the natives they had seen until then had been so skittish. About twenty years earlier, an Englishman named Captain Hunt had tricked some of the local Indians by pretending he wanted to trade and, once he had some twenty warriors on board his ship, he ". . . carried them away and sold them as slaves for twenty pounds a head, like a wretched man that cares not what mischief he doth for his profit." (2)

They met again to conclude the colony business. After barely an hour, right on schedule, Samoset strode out of the woods, followed by four others. (**) He introduced his friend, Squanto, a handsome man in his mid-thirties, a member of the Pautuxet Tribe once located quite near what has since become the Plimouth Plantation. As a young lad, he made himself useful to the crew of an English trading vessel and, when they were ready to return, they invited him to accompany them back to England.

Chapter Seventeen

FINDING CAPTAIN MYLES STANDISH

Samoset and Squanto

Squanto accepted the offer and lived as a servant to the family of Charles Robbins, one of the sailors. After several years, Squanto asked his master to arrange passage back to America as soon as possible. Captain John Smith was not due to sail for some months but he was able to arrange for Squanto to be taken aboard a second ship owned by another captain, John Hunt.

Once he landed in New England, Captain Hunt tricked Squanto and 20 other young Indians into boarding his ship, after which he sailed off to Spain in the year 1614, and sold the men into slavery. Luckily for Squanto, he was purchased by a group of friars at a Catholic monastery. After they freed him, they arranged passage to England where, after three years as a household servant, he was able to obtain passage back to North America. By the time he finally returned home, he had been gone at least a dozen years. Although this was doubtlessly a harsh trial to him at the time, it probably saved his life. When, after great hardship and much good luck, he was able to return home, most of his tribe had perished from the plague. Out of necessity, he joined the Wampanoags.

Perhaps because his English was superior to that of Samoset, the colonists asked Squanto to be their main negotiator with other tribesmen. It soon became obvious that there was much interest on both sides in forging a treaty of friendship, peace and mutual support in the event of an enemy attack.

Samoset and Squanto informed their hosts that the Great Sachem, Massasoit, was camped nearby and intended to visit them on the morrow to propose a friendship treaty. However, a meeting the following day was a problem for the Saints, the next day being the Sabbath. Until now, the ban against non-religious activities, even under the direst of circumstances, had been strictly observed. Surely, they argued, Chief Massasoit could be put off for another day. Some of the Strangers, probably led by their military leader, reminded them that they had waited for such an opportunity for more than three anxious months. Were they now willing to chance offending the main Indian Chieftain and possibly forfeit their friendship, just when it was needed most?

The two intermediaries provided the clinching argument when they explained to the Pilgrims that because of Captain Hunt's earlier treachery, there had recently been severe reprisals. Less than a year earlier, other neighboring Indians had killed three whites in a skirmish with Sir Ferdinando Gorges' Northern Virginia Company. Now, both sides could take steps to avoid a repetition of this unfortunate event by agreeing to a binding peace treaty. Opposition to a Sunday meeting evaporated as preparations for receiving Massasoit took on an entirely new importance. Anyone hoarding even small amounts of food was told to bring it forth. It was make-or-break time for the colonists; nothing could be held back. The problem was that no one knew how many they would have to feed. Ten, twenty, perhaps as many as thirty?

Chapter Seventeen

FINDING CAPTAIN MYLES STANDISH

Samoset and Squanto

Everyone agreed that it had to be done right. For an important occasion such as this, the Indians would expect gifts of more than just trinkets. But more than this, they would be hungry and substantial amounts of good food must be provided. Marksmen were sent out into the woods to search for turkeys and other small game, other hunters went down to the marshes to look for ducks, geese or anything that could be cooked and eaten. No rest at all that night for the Pilgrim women.

(*) Curiously, his election, held on the 25th of March, 1621, actually took place on New Year's Day. This was due to the fact that, before the adoption of the Julian calendar, the beginning of the New Year had gradually shifted to the 25th of March.

(**) Some accounts have Samoset returning two weeks later, not two days. This is not important but mentioned here to make the reader aware that a number of other such discrepancies exist due to the fact that so many historians have included surmises of their own. I have used what seems to be the most likely sequence of events but cannot be sure they are all correct.

Chapter Eighteen

FINDING CAPTAIN MYLES STANDISH

Treaty with Massasoit

Negotiating with Chief Massasoit

A treaty of friendship between the colonists and the neighboring tribes had advantages for both sides. Although the Great Sachem held sway over seven other tribes, ranging from Rhode Island the entire way south to the lands now occupied by the Pilgrims, he was surrounded by Narragansett enemies and his authority was being challenged even within his own tribe. From his standpoint, having the white men with their muskets and cannon as allies was a critical tactical advantage.

The benefits of a friendship pact with Massasoit were of immense value to the colonists as well. They were supposed to be traders—not soldiers—and except for their own sustenance, not farmers, either. The sponsors wanted them to send bales of prime beaver skins and only local natives could be expected to trap them in quantities. This meant that a network of trading posts had to be promptly established. Good relations with the local Indians were vital if they were ever to get free of debt to the Virginia Company.

It was never intended that the colonists would grow all their own food. The sponsors had promised to send foodstuffs in exchange for furs, but the planters were expected to supplement this with homegrown produce. The problem was they had yet to send back so much as one beaver pelt, and in exchange, the Virginia Company had sent them nothing.

Chapter Eighteen

FINDING CAPTAIN MYLES STANDISH

Treaty with Massasoit

Back in England, Captain John Smith had told them much about Indian corn and how valuable it was as a food crop. Now that it was almost time for spring planting, they decided they had better pay for the seed they had earlier taken. But, with the tribe wiped out by the plague, whom were they to pay and with what? Perhaps this could be discussed with Massasoit.

The waiting Pilgrims were stunned and alarmed the next morning when Chief Massasoit arrived at the plantation accompanied by sixty warriors. Why so many? How could they possibly feed all of them?

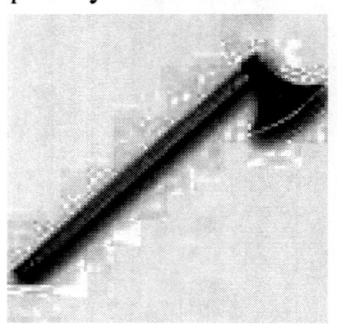

Using a combination of English and sign language, Samoset and Squanto informed the Pilgrims that their great chief—or Sagamores as Bradford calls them—had arrived for a state visit to discuss a treaty of friendship.

Massasoit signaled the Pilgrims to approach. Standish and Squanto met them outside the plantation walls where Standish insisted that they shed themselves of all weapons of war—bows, arrows and knives. As a token of good faith and to further demonstrate their good will, the Indians gave back the tools Standish and Cook thought were gone forever. It was an encouraging start.

Squanto, acting as emissary for his tribe, told the Puritans that fellow tribesmen were still unwilling to expose themselves to what could easily be a clever trap. They demanded that the Pilgrims send a single representative to them for a parley. Now it was the colonists' turn to be wary; they selected a delegate they could best afford to lose; Edward Winslow was given the dubious honor. He carried with him gifts of knives, jewels, biscuits and butter along with some hard water, all of which were "willingly accepted."

Both sides were suspicious of the other but unwilling to let this opportunity pass; there might not be another. "In the end the king left Winslow in the custody of Quadequina, his brother, and came over the brook with some twenty men who left all their bows and arrows behind. The colonists were no fools; "We kept six or seven of them as hostages for our messenger."

Standish took seven musketeers with him down to the brook where they met the warriors, exchanged salutes and then escorted them to one of the unfinished houses. The guests were welcomed, after which they sat on rugs and cushions, Indian style. Governor Carver, although quite unwell, nobly performed the duties of his office and entered with all the pomp he could muster, given his limited wardrobe. English subjects knew how to honor distinguished sovereigns; Governor Carver kissed the hand of Massasoit and the discussions began on a friendly note.

Chapter Eighteen

FINDING CAPTAIN MYLES STANDISH

Treaty with Massasoit

"The governor called for some strong water and drunk to him, and Chief Massasoit drunk a great draught that made him sweat all the while after." They shared freshly killed venison, more "stronge drink" and talked of peace. (2)

After much palaver on both sides, a treaty of peace and friendship was agreed upon. It is doubtful that an agreement such as this could have been achieved without the assistance of Samoset and Squanto.

Massasoit Treaty of Peace, Mutual Aid and Friendship

1. That neither he nor any of his should injure or do hurt to any of our people.

2. And if any of his did hurt to any of ours, he should send the offender, that we might punish him.

3. That if any of our tools were taken away when our people were at work, he should cause them to be restored; and if ours did any harm to any of his; we would do the like to them.

4. If any did unjustly war against him, we would aid him; if any did war against us, he should aid us.

5. He should send to his neighbor confederates to certify them of this that, they might not wrong us but might be likewise comprised in conditions of peace.

6. That when their men came to us they should leave their bows and arrows behind them as we should do our pieces when we came to them.

Chapter Eighteen

FINDING CAPTAIN MYLES STANDISH

Treaty with Massasoit

Just as before, it was almost as hard to get rid of the visitors as it had been to establish contact with them. First, the colonists ceremoniously escorted Massasoit back to his camp. Then, the ceremony was repeated for his brother, Quadequina. That over, several Indians indicated they wanted to return and spend the night. Fat chance; Squanto and Samoset alone were allowed this privilege.

Before parting, the Indians vowed that in eight or nine days they would return to help the settlers plant corn in the field opposite the brook. After withdrawing a short distance into the woods, they made camp with their women and children just near enough to keep the wary Pilgrims on the alert all night long.

Early the next morning some of the tribesmen were back at the plantation expecting to be fed. They let it be known that Massasoit desired still more parley. "Captain Standish and Isaac Allerton went virtuously and were welcomed by him after his manner. He gave them three or four ground nuts and some tobacco." The friendliness of the Indians and lack of hostility pleased and relieved the Planters. Some of them began to wonder if it might not be time to set aside their skepticism. "We cannot yet conceive but that he is willing peace with us. They have seen our people in the woods sometimes two or three alone at work and fowling when as they offered them no harm, as they might easily have done."

There was another reason why the Indians wanted to be friends with the white man: ". . . we are especially encouraged to believe this because he (Massasoit) hath a potent adversary, the Narragansett that are at war with them. Against these he thinks we may be some strength to him, for our pieces are terrible unto them." (2)

The Indians continued to overstay their welcome, remaining well into late morning. Something had to be done; Governor Carver finally told them to bring an iron kettle to the plantation where ". . . we filled it full of peas, which pleased them well. However, by the end of June, the colonists had been visited by so many Indian delegations expecting to be entertained and fed that it became necessary for the colonists to send emissaries forth to ask them to desist lest they run out of food for themselves. With Squanto as guide, the reliable Edward Winslow and Stephen Hopkins set off to accomplish this delicate task. While enroute, they were accosted by a dozen Indians who followed them for miles, insisting on gifts of trinkets or food.

Winslow and Hopkins walked the forest path for nearly forty miles and, while doing so, had to give away what little food they had with them. The hungry, weary travelers naturally expected to be fed by their hosts, but there was no food offered and the next day they were nearly famished before they made their way back to the plantation.

Chapter Eighteen

FINDING CAPTAIN MYLES STANDISH

Treaty with Massasoit

It was from this shaky beginning, that the Colony came under the protection of Massasoit, a benefit that lasted until his death, some 20 years later. It probably spared them all from being massacred during the Pequot War of 1836, and doubtlessly kept them from almost certain starvation during their early years at Plymouth.

Squanto and Samoset remained with the colonists to provide them with counsel and advice on everything they needed to know to survive in the New England wilderness. Samoset became a life-long friend and servant to Myles Standish. Squanto did not live long afterwards; within two years he became sick and died while visiting a neighboring tribe, probably from the white man's plague.

When Chief Massasoit died, his eldest son Wamsutta (Alexander) succeeded him, but he also died a short time afterwards. Metacom (Philip) assumed his brother's place. In 1675, he began what has become known as King Phillip's War, Colonial historian Francis Jennings estimates that nearly 7 of every 8 Native Americans and 6 of every 13 English settlers were killed, making it proportionately the bloodiest war ever fought on the North American continent.

For the rest of his short life, Squanto would continue to play an important role in Colony affairs, staying with them for about 18 months. During that time, he helped them in many important ways, but his association with the white men seems to have gone to his head. He foolishly attempted to stage a leadership coup, unsuccessfully contesting the authority of Chief Massasoit, the very man who took him in as a full member of the Wampanoag Tribe when he came back to America to find himself the only surviving member of his own tribe.

Understandably, Squanto was no longer welcome as a Wampanoag and regarded as an unreliable ally by the colonists, since his actions very nearly caused their Treaty of Friendship with the Wampanoags to die aborning.

However, Squanto had been very helpful to the Pilgrims, showing them how to build warmer houses and taught them when and how to plant corn on a small mound of soil, with a fish buried with the seeds as fertilizer. Without his help, they never would have been able to grow almost 20 acres of valuable corn that first summer.

Chapter Eighteen

FINDING CAPTAIN MYLES STANDISH

Treaty with Massasoit

He also showed them how to capture eels by trodding them out of the low-tide shoreline mud with his feet and catching them with his bare hands. They were all amazed when he returned one evening "with as many as he could well lift in one hand, which our people were glad of—they were fat and sweet."

But Squanto's efforts (also known as Tisquantum) to assist the colonists came to an untimely end, when in November of 1622, while on a trading mission to the Massachusetts Indians, Squanto came down with "Indian fever," as it was then called. His nose began to bleed excessively and he soon died. His passing was regretted by many, but not all, of his white friends.

Chapter Nineteen

FINDING CAPTAIN MYLES STANDISH

The Standish Monument

Thee limbs that cannot move, the eyes that cannot see,
These are not entirely me.
Dead men and women helped to shape the mold
Which I do not escape; the words
I speak, my written line; these are not uniquely mine.
For in my heart and in my will
Old ancestors are warring still.
Celt, Roman, Saxon and all the dead
From whose rich blood my veins are fed,
In aspect, gesture, voices, tone,
Flesh of my flesh, bone of my bone;
In fields they tilled I plow the sod,
I walk the mountain paths they trod;
And round my daily steps arise
The good and bad of those I comprise.
~ Richard Rolle

Chapter Nineteen

FINDING CAPTAIN MYLES STANDISH

The Standish Monument

The next morning, we visited the Standish Monument high atop what is still known as Captain's Hill. The fifteen-foot statue of Myles Standish can be seen from twenty miles away. It seems ironic that Myles, well known for his diminutive size, should be commemorated by a statue three times his actual height, but then on reflection, his stature in life was also triple-sized. His memorial is mounted atop a one-hundred and forty-foot granite column from which he forever gazes across the bay where the Mayflower first anchored so many years ago.

Due to the Massachusetts park system budget problems, we found the massive Iron Gate at the bottom of Captain's Hill closed to auto traffic. A minor inconvenience such as this was not going to deter us. We parked our car and began the hike up the long, winding drive. As we huffed our way up the incline, I thought about the ceremonies that had taken place when the monument and park were dedicated in 1871, the 150th anniversary of the Mayflower landing. According to newspapers of the day, the dedication ceremony was a major national event attended by hundreds of distinguished citizens from all over the country. They came to Duxbury by steamboat and a specially chartered train. Upon their arrival, mounted honor guards escorted the dignitaries to the dedication site. They came from Washington, New York and Boston. One-hundred-gun salutes thundered in honor of the long-departed hero. According to the custom of the day, lengthy tributes were delivered by long-winded orators, all of them extolling praises of the first commissioned officer in the New World. A local newspaper of the day describes this momentous event:

> "The first train on the new Duxbury and Cohasset Railroad arrived at the Duxbury station at seven o'clock the evening previous, with freight and passengers, and bringing a section of two guns and twenty men of the First Battery. On the morning of the seventeenth, on the arrival of the cars and steamboat, the Exercises of The Day commenced with the firing of one hundred guns by the battery. A procession was formed at the depot, under the direction of Joshua M. Cushing, the Marshal of The Day, the Standish Guards, Lt. Lanman, commanding, acting as Escort."

In the flowery oratorical traditions of the day, the speaker commenced his "short recital" of the life and deeds of the honored captain. It being the middle of August, it was probably quite warm, even hot. The audience would have been in the unshaded, open air and the chairs they sat upon of the wooden, folding variety; hard and uncomfortable. The oration that follows below has been mercifully edited to perhaps one-third of its original length. It is worth reading, if only so one can marvel at the stamina of the audience; how long would a modern-day crowd stay under such circumstances?

Chapter Nineteen

FINDING CAPTAIN MYLES STANDISH

The Standish Monument

EXERCISES OF CONSECRATION ON CAPTAIN'S HILL

August 17, 1871

Oration by Gn. Horace Binney Sergeant

It would have been more fitting to the grandeur of a noble memory that a distinguished connection of Myles Standish should have addressed you to-day. . . I crave your courteous patience for my short recital of a well-known story, and my reverent tribute to a life supremely brave. Elizabeth signed his commission as lieutenant in the English forces, serving in the Netherlands against the cruel armies of the Inquisition. As she died in 1603, about two years after his majority, it is not improbable that we are indebted to that first disappointment, which may have driven him, in his early manhood and some despair, into the army.

From 1600 to 1609 . . . the contest was peculiarly obstinate and bloody. In this fierce school, the Puritan Captain learned the temper and art of war. From 1609 to 1620 the Low Countries were inflamed by theological disputes...and, in this school, perhaps, Myles Standish learned some uncompromising religious opinions, which brought him in to strange sympathy and connection with the Pilgrim church in Leyden. Both periods seemed to leave their impress on his character. The inventory, recorded with his will, mentions the Commentaries of Caesar, Bariffe's Artillery, three old Bibles and three muskets, with the harness of time, complete. . . When, in obedience to the colonial orders to crush a great Indian conspiracy, he took a squad of eight picked men into the forests, and deemed it prudent to kill the most turbulent warrior with his own hand . . . to stab Pecksuot to the heart with his own knife; a giant who had taunted him with his small stature in almost the very words of Goliath, in his insulting sneer at David, long before; and to cut off the head of Wituwamat, which bloody trophy the elders had ordered him to bring home with him. . .The materials for personal biography are scanty.

Chapter Nineteen

FINDING CAPTAIN MYLES STANDISH

The Standish Monument

His wife, Rose Standish—an English rose—whose very name augurs unfitness for a New-England winter on an unsettled cape, died within a month of the landing. A light tradition exists that his second wife, Barbara, was her sister, whom he left an orphan child in England, and sent for. She arrived a woman grown, and the valorous captain added another illustration to the poet's story. From the first anchorage, Captain Standish, as the soldier of the company, was charged with all deeds of adventure. . .his repute in affairs, both civil and military, was such that he was for many years the treasurer of the colony, and, during a period of difficulty, their agent in England. . . it seems to me providential for the colonists that one of their number was, by temper and training, unable to sympathize with that soft tenderness for human life which is wont to characterize saintly-mined men, like the Rev. Mr Robinson, who, when he heard of the marvelous conflict where Standish, with three of four others, in a locked room, killed the same number of hostile chiefs that were gathering their tribes to exterminate the English, uttered these sorrowful words: "Oh! That you had converted some before you killed any!"

It was fortunate of us who believe in Plymouth Rock, that one trained soldier came out in the Mayflower. Had the fate of the Pilgrims depended on such motives, Elder Brewster and his company would have been buried like the earlier explorer, the son of Eric the Red, and American civilization might have been for centuries deferred.
. . . if Myles Standish had not been a trained soldier, the revered heirs of the elders of the little church of Leyden would probably have adorned the wigwams of "the Massachusetts."

Once atop the monument hill, impressed by the spectacular view, I shot an entire roll of film—or so I thought. I varied shutter speeds in order to be certain of getting the best possible view of Standish on his pedestal, the beautiful harbor and the blue ocean beyond. We walked the quarter mile back down the hill to our automobile where I discovered there was no film in my camera. Out of respect for Puritan sensibilities, I refrained from even the mildest profanity and simply went back up the hill, imagining another, somewhat smaller figure, probably in much better physical condition, making his way up the hill to look for a cow, fetch his sheep, or perhaps just to enjoy the view.

Chapter Nineteen

FINDING CAPTAIN MYLES STANDISH

The Standish Monument

Standish homestead

Not long after his death in 1656, Myles's house was destroyed by fire and was never rebuilt, at least not on the same site. It seems that the beautiful beachfront Myles had enjoyed so much was problematic due to the destructive wave action caused by frequent Atlantic storms. After salvaging some of the heavier timbers from his father's old house, Alexander built his dwelling a few hundred yards further inland on a spot more protected from the wrath of the stormy Atlantic.

A small depression in the ground is all that remains of the original Standish home, a root or perhaps a storm cellar and marked by two stones place at either end to commemorate the spot where the house had been. A few simple comments etched into a plain granite boulder identify the spot, nothing more. Myles had constructed his home, a long, rectangular structure, on a thirty-foot bluff where he could look across the bay to see Plymouth Plantation and perhaps monitor the comings and goings of ships in the harbor. Originally, Myles's house was much farther away from the bluff's edge, but over the intervening years, relentless ocean waves have eroded much of the land that once separated house from shore.

Chapter Nineteen

FINDING CAPTAIN MYLES STANDISH

The Standish Monument

A short distance down a narrow footpath toward the beach, we found a small bronze tablet marking the spot where once a spring, now dormant, supplied the family with its drinking water. Nearby, what was once Myles's farmland is now sub-divided into streets named after Mayflower passengers. Priscilla Lane is but a stone's throw away from the entrance to Alexander's cottage. Considering the historical setting, the local residents' bicycles, motorcycles and pick-up trucks seemed entirely out of place. Pedestrians only, I thought.

We next visited the cottage Alexander Standish built in 1666; according to the date carved on the massive fireplace mantle. The cottage is well back from the street, hidden from view and not open to tourists. However, we were told by passers-by that the present owner was no longer in residence, and if we would simply drive in, take a quick look and then leave, no one would mind. After making certain that my camera was properly loaded, we drove down the entrance lane and were astonished to discover how well preserved the old structure was. This has not always been so. The following editorial is from a Plymouth area newspaper editorial dated sometime after 1871.

> No name in American history stands for greater courage and fearlessness, for greater boldness and more intrepid daring than the name of the man who had not the courage to speak for himself and ask the woman of his choice to be his wife. . . But Myles Standish was nevertheless as brave a man as ever buckled a sword, and we do well to bear his name in grateful remembrance. . . In Pilgrim hall at Plymouth may be seen his sword and other articles once belonging to him. And on Duxbury hill is the famous old Standish house, built in 1666, as is stated in entirely legible characters on the great chimney. The house was not built by Myles Standish, but by his son Alexander about ten years after his death. . . The house belonged to four generations of the Standish Family since which time it has had various owners. It is now the property of a Mr. Allen, who does not occupy it, nor has it been occupied for some years. The windows are boarded up and an air of desolation surrounds the old house.

Chapter Nineteen

FINDING CAPTAIN MYLES STANDISH

The Standish Monument

> John Alden and his wife Priscilla, were without doubt, frequent visitors at the house, as Alexander Standish was married to John Alden's daughter, Sarah, and it is certain that not only John and Priscilla Alden, but many others of the Mayflower Pilgrims have crossed the threshold of this ancient house which ought to be preserved as one of the sacred landmarks of American history.
> (Name of newspaper unknown)

Obviously, the newspaper appeal was effective, or perhaps local civic organizations came through with special fund-raising efforts. In any event, the cottage restoration folks did their work very well. Even though it is now well over two centuries old, the Alexander Standish house could easily be mistaken for a shingle-covered cottage of, say, early to mid 1900 vintage. I took several quick photos, and not wanting to alarm the neighbors, we departed to visit the cemetery where the Captain lies in final repose after being disinterred twice to confirm the grave's authenticity, its resident for many years having been the subject of local speculation.

Chapter Twenty

FINDING CAPTAIN MYLES STANDISH

Ashfield, Massachusetts

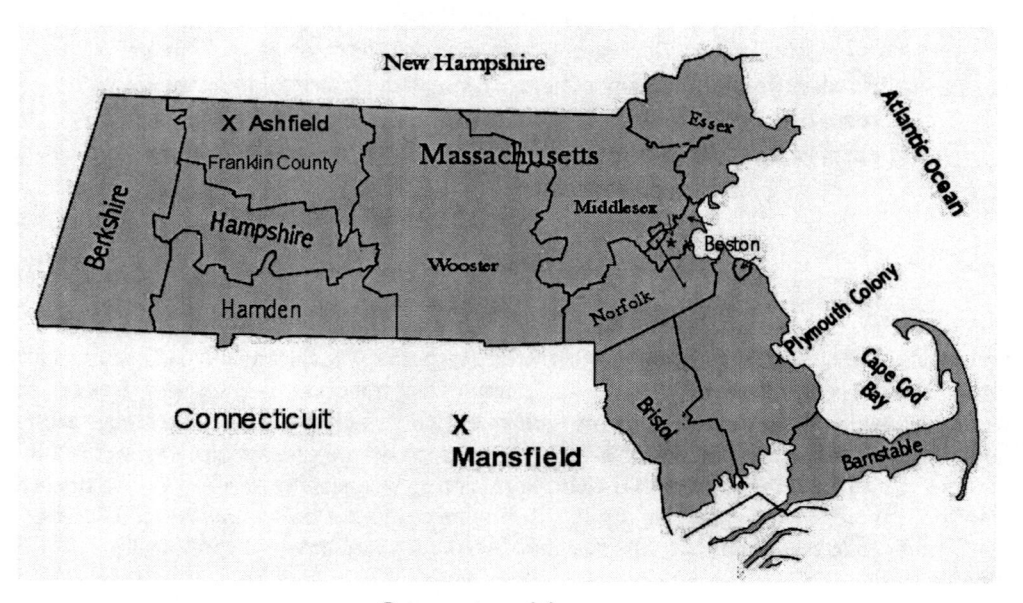

Our eastern itinerary

The first week of our eastern research trip had been extremely interesting, even fascinating, but we still had not found what we had most hoped to discover—a document of record proving that Amie Standish Young was the daughter of Israel Standish of Ashfield, Massachusetts.

Although I was, by now, fairly certain that she was wrong about this, an earlier Young family researcher, Ione Cumberland, now deceased, had written in her 1949 Young Family History that Amie Standish Young was buried in Ashfield. This contradicted what I had recently been told by Walter Young, of Elkhart, but it was intriguing enough to cause an early morning stroll through the Ashfield cemetery. Ruth and I walked slowly up and down every row of headstones and looked carefully at each. Many of them were very ancient and hard to read but we found neither Standishes nor Youngs. On our way east a week earlier, Walter had pointed out what he believed was Amie's gravestone in the Beaver Dam Cemetery but the tombstone markings were barely legible and it was still an open question. So, although Amie was supposed to be buried in two separate places, I was not able to be positive of either.

Chapter Twenty

FINDING CAPTAIN MYLES STANDISH

Ashfield, Massachusetts

Museum curator, Mrs. Hall, and the Society's Genealogical Researcher, Martha Townsley, welcomed us at the door. Mrs. Townsley said that she already "knew" me. She explained that, just a few days earlier she had received a letter I had sent to the Society the previous November, five months earlier. She explained that for most of the past year, the Society had been in a state of upheaval with the installation of a new floor and the retirement of the previous curator. Apparently, my letter requesting information about the Standishes and the Youngs had been shuffled about until it was finally passed to Mrs. Townsley. Since then, she had been very busy assembling an impressive assortment of records and many old books of Ashfield history. We spent several hours examining them with her, finding many interesting bits of information, but nothing new about the people we had come to research.

One of the museum books was particularly interesting to me: "The History of Ashfield Massachusetts—from its Settlement in 1742 to 1910," by Frederick G. Howe, published in 1919. The preface of the book explained that at a 1908 Ashfield town meeting, it was decided that "a town history be published" and explained that such a task was possible because the town records had been so well preserved. It was further decided that the town's history would feature one particular manuscript written by a local historian in 1840, seventy years previously, "when early events were fresh in the minds of the older people then living."

Howe's book contained several references to the Standish family, and although the information given about them was already familiar to me, the book provided a fascinating look at life in pioneer Ashfield when the Standishes came to the area. When I expressed regret that the book was no longer in print, Mrs. Townsley was pleased to tell me that the Society had just recently undertaken the sponsorship of a second printing. I promptly ordered a copy, which I have since received. It has been a valuable resource for this work.

Earlier, I had noted that after Israel died, some of his descendants relocated from Ashfield to New York State, causing me to wonder what prompted these moves since it seemed they had all married locally. After reading Mr Howe's book, I better understood the reason; a great many Ashfield citizens of that era had also relocated to New York, all because of their desire to cash in on the popularity of the aromatic peppermint plant.

According to author Howe, the oil of peppermint had become not only a fashionable and widely used cooking condiment but also a valuable aromatic. The technique of commercially extracting and bottling this fragrant essence was developed by Ashfield entrepreneurs and had become an extremely lucrative business about the time Israel Standish died in 1804. The peppermint extract was sold door-to-door by an army of young men who regularly left Ashfield with backpacks filled with small bottles of peppermint oil and various other household notions. However, we have not been able to establish if any Standishes were among them.

Chapter Twenty

FINDING CAPTAIN MYLES STANDISH

Ashfield, Massachusetts

Competition from New York peppermint growers began to take its toll and gradually many Ashfield families left for more productive farmlands. In the 1810 census, the Ashfield population reached its zenith at 1809 citizens, forty years later in 1850, only 1394 remained. The last of the Standishes had left the area by 1820.

When I inquired if anyone at the Historical Society could help us find a place called Baptist Corners, where the Standishes had once lived, everyone there knew exactly where it was, but then suggested we get in touch with Norma Harris, the former curator of the museum. All agreed that she was the single most knowledgeable person to have along on a mission such as ours. They were absolutely right.

Upon receiving my phone call asking for a meeting, Mrs. Harris invited us to come to her home the following morning for coffee. She lived in a wooded area a mile or so beyond the village limits. We found her to be a most charming lady with encyclopedic knowledge about Ashfield and its residents, past and present, exactly the kind of person we had hoped to find.

After receiving my call the night before, Mrs. Harris had spent the balance of the evening assembling an impressive amount of information about the Standish family. However, it was not what I had been hoping for. Her sources were the very same Ashfield Vital Records I had previously received months earlier from the County Clerk's office, wherein no Amy was listed as one of Israel Standish's daughters.

There were three main issues we hoped to resolve during our Ashfield visit: Firstly, when and where Israel and his wife, Elizabeth, were married. "Ashfield Marriages" shows that Israel Standish and Elisabeth "Partarich" (Patrick, Partridge) filed their "Intentions to marry" in 1764, as was the custom in those days, but there seems to be no record of the actual ceremony. Why not?

Secondly; "Ashfield Births" lists Israel and Sara (h) as the parents of Jerusha (1765); Sara (h) (1767); Elizabeth (1770); and Israel (1773). This has to be incorrect. Although Israel did eventually marry a woman named Sarah after Elizabeth died 1792, he did so two years later. The Sarah referred to here had to be the widow Sarah Harvey, a next-door neighbor.

Thirdly, according to several earlier Young family researchers, Amy Standish had been born in Ashfield in 1780 and married a man named John Young before 1802. However, neither had provided any documentation; perhaps one had used the other as a source? We were again disappointed. There was no record of Amy's birth, marriage or of giving birth to children. Were we barking up the wrong family tree?

Chapter Twenty-one

FINDING CAPTAIN MYLES STANDISH

Baptist Corners

The Arvidson / Standish farm, 1990 photo

The next morning we picked up Mrs. Harris at her home so she could guide us to the old Standish farm at Baptist Corners. She knew the present owners and said she had telephoned for permission to bring a Standish descendant to their farm for a short visit. They said they would be pleased to have us come, and of course, we were delighted be allowed to visit.

The winding rural road had once been surfaced with a thin coating of blacktop, but it was now quite full of holes that had been patched, patch upon patch and best driven slowly. A leisurely pace suited us just fine, allowing us an opportunity to better view our surroundings as we made our way to Baptist Corners. Having grown up in the area, Mrs. Harris knew many of the old farm occupants along the way and she shared with us a wealth of local histories as we bumped and thumped our way along.

Our guide was much bothered by the manner in which some of the old farms had been allowed to fall into disrepair. A one-time farmer herself, she knew how hard the old settlers had worked to clear the land and to her mind, it seemed shameful that the current residents, most of them weekend commuters, did not do more to keep the woods and weeds from taking over. Ruth and I did not mind this aspect of the scenic countryside we were enjoying but we, of course, kept that opinion to ourselves.

Chapter Twenty-one

FINDING CAPTAIN MYLES STANDISH

Baptist Corners

At Mrs. Harris's direction, we turned northeast on the old Baptist Corner road where she pointed out the spot where each of the original buildings of the Baptist Corners settlement had once stood; all of them now long since gone.

Although Baptist Corners presently exists mainly as a historical footnote to those with an appreciation of early Ashfield history, it was a fascinating experience for us; here was the neighborhood where Israel once lived and where he married and raised his family. We wondered what stories we would hear if we could talk to the spirits we could almost feel hovering about us.

Baptist Corners is well worth a visit. Anyone wishing to find it has only to stop and ask directions at the Ashfield Historical Society or, if it is not open, from almost any local resident as it is generally well known. It is located less than ten miles from Ashfield. However, even with directions, Baptist Corners would be easy to miss; one has to look closely to see, here and there, the remains of a foundation where the Baptist Church or the Baptist Corners School had been. It being mid-summer, the area was quite grown over and the old settlement blended seamlessly into wild meadows and encroaching woodlands.

Our navigator knew precisely where most of the old buildings had stood. She pointed out to us the foundation of the school where Jerusha, Sarah, Elizabeth, Israel Jr., and, as we were soon able to prove, our 4th great-grandmother, Amie and sister Submit, had been educated.

Several hundred yards west of where the school had been, we turned into the entrance of the old Israel Standish farm. A narrow gravel driveway inclined up a gentle grade to the home of Pat and Nordahl Arvidson, both of them waiting for us at the crest of the slope. The Arvidsons seemed to be just as pleased to receive us as we were to be there. They had purchased the property seventeen years earlier and it was obvious that they have worked very hard to make it a lovely place to live.

The Arvidsons were justly proud of what they had done with the land and the buildings. It had not been possible to preserve all the ancient features but, considering the age and condition of what they had to work with, they had done remarkably well.

The house was T-shaped, with the short stem of the T being the original Standish cabin and, of course, the oldest part of the house. The long, cross-portion of the T had been added much later, probably in the mid-to-late 1800's. The Arvidsons would have preferred to leave the logs in the kitchen exposed in their original condition, but because the rough bark surface was attractive to insects and was impossible to keep even reasonably clean, they regretfully covered most of them with wood paneling, leaving exposed just selected portions of the original cedar beams in the ceiling.

Chapter Twenty-one

FINDING CAPTAIN MYLES STANDISH

Baptist Corners

In order to better preserve it, the original log exterior of the cabin portion had been sheathed in white aluminum siding, thus blending it into the rest of the house but giving no hint to a passer-by of its age or history. The cabin portion of the house serves as a combination kitchen-family room, with a large picture window that overlooks what had been the old farmyard and the fields and pasture beyond. Also visible is a well-tended green lawn divided by a flower-lined lane leading up to what was once Israel's 27-acre orchard.

Running parallel along either side of this narrow lane was an ancient stone fence, probably built when the land was first cleared. Its only use now was to serve as a reminder of the labor required to turn this stoney, thin-soiled property into a farm capable of being tilled for the growing of crops, fodder, vegetables and flowers.

Like other such fences throughout the area, each stone had been carefully placed to maintain its integrity as a barrier to livestock, either to keep them out or keep them in. In the intervening years when horses and cattle were no longer kept on the property, the fence had been allowed to deteriorate as one stone and then another shifted position in response to time, the heaving of winter frost, benign neglect, and the pull of gravity.

Beyond the old barn, a large field could be seen, bordered by woods, with rolling hills in the background, a picture-postcard setting. When they bought the property, the previous owner told the Arvidsons that it had once belonged to a relative of Myles Standish, but he didn't know more than that. Although much interested in the Standish connection, the Arvidsons had never researched the matter, thinking it would be impossible to do so this long after the fact. Our hosts were, therefore, especially pleased to learn that it was the 3rd and 4th great-grandsons of Captain Myles Standish that had once owned their property and built the original buildings. I was pleased to be able to present them with copies of several land records to verify what I had just told them.

Mr. Arvidson called my attention to what was obviously a very old pear tree growing nearby, telling me that the previous owner had claimed that when he purchased the property many years earlier it was a very old tree then. His comment triggered a recollection, and upon returning home, I re-read Nora Fenno's, "As I Remember It." Nora's reminiscences of life on Alonzo Young's farm in Erie County, Pennsylvania mentions her grandfather bringing pear seeds with him when he relocated from Ashfield to Amity Township:

> "They set out a nice orchard and grandfather brought Pear seed from his native state Mass. and planted it in the Orchard. The Pear tree is now standing and bears the grandest fruit every year."
>
> Nora Fenno

Chapter Twenty-one

FINDING CAPTAIN MYLES STANDISH

Baptist Corners

The barn dates back to the 1700's, according to a professional "sawmill historian" who told the Arvidsons that, because of the manner it was sawn and the two inch thickness of the original planks, he was confident that it had been built in the late 1700's, conveniently coinciding with the arrival in the area of Miles and his family. The old barn had been extremely well built with solid, hand-hewn beams and well-mortised joints, but the roof had deteriorated badly by the time it was acquired by the Arvidsons and required a great deal of work to restore. The exterior barn planking had never been painted, and after a century and a half of weathering, the two-inch rough-sawn cedar planks had become much thinner than they once were and in danger of splitting. In order to prevent further deterioration, Nordahl regretfully painted the building a traditional "barn red." Although his reason for doing so was explained as being the only available alternative, I could not help but wish he had instead treated it with a clear wood preservative that would have maintained its aged appearance and more of its intrinsic historical value.

Perhaps sensing my unspoken thoughts and wanting to put the painting of the old barn on a happier plane, Mr. Arvidson invited me to step inside the barn with him, where after some rummaging through a small pile of remnant boards, he produced a short length of the original, badly eroded, unpainted pine plank. He presented it to me as a gift which I have since caused to be appropriately engraved. It hangs on our library wall, a much-cherished souvenir of the old Standish farmstead.

Stone-lined lane leading to fields and pasture

Chapter Twenty-one

FINDING CAPTAIN MYLES STANDISH

Baptist Corners

One of the more attractive features of the old farmyard was the flowerbed on either side of a narrow stone lane that once guided livestock from barn to pasture. Miles and Israel probably built this low stone fence, which was about sixty feet in length. This stonewalled lane led to a wooded area just beyond the barnyard. It was probably the escape route used by the Standishes when they fled into the woods to hide from what they thought was a menacing band of Indians.

According to local lore passed along from one owner to the next, the family was about to sit down to a meal when a sizeable group of Indians was seen approaching the farm. Very aware that not many years earlier, a marauding band had massacred a number of families in a community less than twenty miles distant, the Standishes fled out a back door and escaped into the nearby woodlot. Fully expecting their home and farm buildings to be set afire, they were surprised when it did not happen. After a time, they returned to find the Indians gone and their possessions intact except for a missing meal and an assortment of foodstuffs and other staples.

View of the old Standish barn from nearby slope

Chapter Twenty-one

FINDING CAPTAIN MYLES STANDISH

Baptist Corners

Nordahl and I walked up to the top of a nearby hill, where he pointed out another stone fence that separates his property from a much larger neighboring field lying just beyond. Obviously, it was where Israel's orchard had been. The day was bright and sunny, with just a few shadows from the clouds drifting slowly eastward across the valley below. Looking down over the old Standish farmstead, I resolved to return some day, perhaps in the fall when the leaves were in full glory.

At the time of our visit with the Arvidsons, neither they nor we realized that there had been an earlier Young family researcher, who had been to their farm long before they purchased it. We later acquired the following essay written in 1949 by Ada Ball Cass of Wisconsin Rapids.

Because this is being written some eighteen years after her son gave me Ada's entire collection of notes and essays, I cannot recall how I first heard about her or obtained her son's address. I do recall driving to his home in Wisconsin Rapids, however, and how surprised I was when he insisted I take the entire file home with me. "No one here is interested," he said.

At the time, this attitude was beyond my understanding but I have since learned that this is something we family historians learn to accept; some are very interested in their antecedents, others could not care less. Fortunately, this "don't care" attitude tends to skip generations.

A Descendant of Captain Myles Standish

In June 1949, the author and family visited the place at Ashfield where Israel and Miles had built their home and lived. The woman living on the farm related an interesting account of an Indian raid upon the Standish family as she had heard it years before from a woman then past ninety years of age. The family was about to eat its meal when a band of Indians appeared. They left the house and fled over the hill into the woods, expecting to see their buildings destroyed. However, that did not happen and when they thought it safe, they returned and found that only the food which had been prepared and the stores of provision had been taken. This was an especially interesting story, because the kitchen of the house on the premises was a part of the original house built by Israel. Another old building, the barn, had been there since the time of the first settlement, and it was known by the children around the neighborhood as "Myles Standish."

Ada Ball Cass

Chapter Twenty-one

FINDING CAPTAIN MYLES STANDISH

Baptist Corners

We did not yet know that the very next day we would discover several documents that would prove beyond a shadow of doubt that Amie Standish was indeed the daughter of Israel and therefore a descendant of Captain Myles, just as Grandmother Tory had said all along. Shame on me for doubting her.

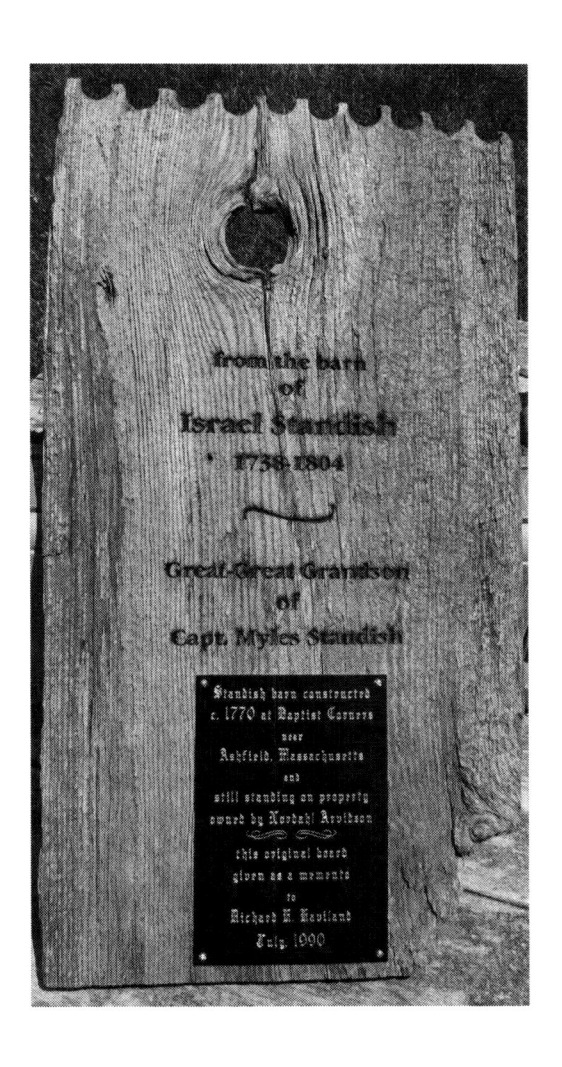

From the Barn
of
Israel Standish (1738-1804)

Great-Great Grandson
of
Captain Myles Standish

Standish barn constructed 1770 at Baptist Corners and still standing on property
Owned by Nordahl Arvidson

This original board given as a memento to Richard H. Haviland
July, 1990

Chapter Twenty-two

FINDING CAPTAIN MYLES STANDISH

Finding Amie and Submit

Earlier, while on our way to Plymouth, we identified the site of grandson Miles Standish's home in Mansfield Hollow and knew that he had relocated from there to Ashfield when his son, Israel, was an infant. It amused us to think how we would have startled our pioneer ancestors out of their wits, had we whizzed by them at that speed while they plodded along with their oxen carts.

After uncovering nothing really new at Plymouth, Duxbury or Ashfield that verified Amie Standish as a daughter of Israel, we decided to make our next stop at Greenfield, the Franklin County seat. We were a bit discouraged however, since we knew that early New England birth, marriage and death records were normally kept at the township, not the county level.

Ashfield was once a part of neighboring Hampshire County and we thought we might also need to go there as well, but as it turned out, we did not. We found what we were looking for at the office of the Greenfield Register of Deeds, where a very helpful woman practically turned her office over to us, including the use of her desk.

She then spent the next hour bringing out ancient volumes of handwritten indexes to early court records. Initially, we found nothing, but fortunately, the dear lady thought of yet one more place to look. After a few minutes, she reappeared with a small metal box taken from an interior, seldom-used vault, apparently restricted to the very oldest documents. While it did not have any of the birth, marriage or death certificates we hoped to find, it did contain the proof we needed of Amie's parentage. In a very ancient envelope, we were delighted to gaze upon the 1806 probate records from the estate of Israel Standish, late of Ashfield. (A will is probated by the court to ensure the wishes of the deceased are faithfully executed).

Chapter Twenty-two

FINDING CAPTAIN MYLES STANDISH

Finding Amie and Submit

The clerk, almost as excited as we were, escorted us to another chamber where we carefully removed and examined a set of papers, all of them in extremely fragile condition. Although I was, of course, pleased to examine them, I could not help but wonder at the wisdom of allowing the public—amateurs such as me—access to such irreplaceable documents. Then I realized that, in this case, we were probably one of the very few to have ever done so.

Carefully, very carefully, we opened the folded parchment-like papers and spread them out on a large conference table. To our untrained eyes, the 185 year-old, quill-written document was quite unreadable, but not to our eager assistant; she at once began reading the first page aloud. Except for a small smudge at one corner of the page, we were assured the writing was entirely legible.

The clerk set the first page aside to make room for the second. Even before she resumed her reading, our eyes went directly to the names at the bottom of the page. There before us, was the proof for which we—and others—had been searching for so long, the proof that Amie Standish was indeed the daughter of Israel, the son of Miles, the son of Israel, etc.

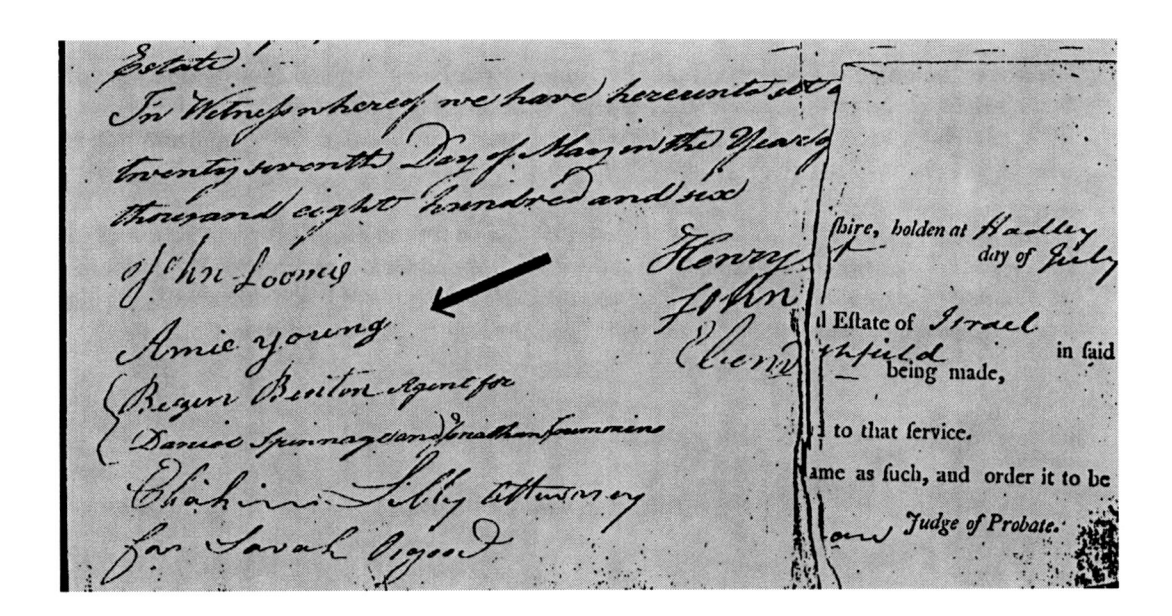

Amie Young's signature on her father's probate document

Chapter Twenty-two

FINDING CAPTAIN MYLES STANDISH

Finding Amie and Submit

All along we had been looking for Amy's birth record but this was just as good, in that it was legal proof that she was Israel's daughter. The purpose of a probate is to divide the deceased's property according to his wishes, and clearly Amie was one of his heirs. For the first time, we realized that her name was not Amy, but, as she signed it herself, "Amie."

This is also the first indication that Amie Young resided, not in Amity, where her father had lived, but in the neighboring township of Conway, where we were told, the town hall had gone up in flames many years ago, perhaps explaining why we had been unable to locate any record of her marriage to John Young.

Also listed on the probate document was Submit, Amie's next oldest sister. Until then, we were unaware of her existence she, as with Amie, was not recorded anywhere in Ashfield vital records. The copy of Israel's probate document on the preceding page shows just the portion that contains, among others, the signature of Amie Young. Also, note that one of the witnesses is a John Alden, doubtless a descendant of Priscilla and John Alden, of Plimouth Plantation, further evidence of the lasting friendship between the Alden and Standish families that carried on for at least five generations and spanned nearly two hundred years after the landing of the Mayflower.

We were, of course very pleased that after years of searching, we had finally found the proof that completed the missing link between our 3rd great-grandmother and Captain Myles Standish. But it was, in a way, almost anti-climactic. There were no bells, no drum rolls, not even a celebratory high-five.

While thanking the Franklin County Register of Deeds for the excellent cooperation of his office staff, I mentioned my concern about the fragility of the documents I had examined. He agreed and explained that every year he requests funds to have all such documents digitized and each year the county board removes it from the budget. Some things never change.

Text of the Probated Record of Israel Standish

Ashfield May 27th 1806

We the Subscribers having been duly appointed to appraise and divide the real Estate of Israel Standish late of said Ashfield deceased have appraised said Estate as follows, Viz.

Chapter Twenty-two

FINDING CAPTAIN MYLES STANDISH

Finding Amie and Submit

One Lot of land at one hundred fifty nine Dollars ninety cents	$159.90
One other Lot of Land at one hundred thirty three Dollars eight cents	$133.08
One Lot of Land at one hundred eighty two dollars thirty seven cents	$ 82.37
The Orchard two hundred fifty two Dollars	$252.00
Two ninth Parts of one Pew in the Baptist meeting House In said Town at two Dollars	$ 2.00
Whole sum Seven hundred & twenty nine Dollars and thirty five Cents	729.35

Finding it very inconvenient to divide said Parcels of Land equally among the Heirs We have assigned to Jerusha Spinnage Daughter to said Israel the following Piece of Land, Viz. A part of said Israel's Homestead and is bounded as follows beginning at a Stake and Stones by the Stone Wall near the Road thence East eighteen Degrees South thirty three Rods to a Stake and Stones—thence North Eighteen Degrees East forty Rods and nineteen links to a Stake and Stones thence West thirteen Degrees. North forty three Rods and three Quarters of a Rod to a stake and Stones—thence South seven Degrees East twenty one Rods to a stake and Stones—thence Southerly by the Stone Wall twenty Rods—thence South fourteen Degrees West twenty Rods to a Stake and Stones—thence West fourteen Degrees South twelve Rods to a stake and Stones—thence West six Degrees North fifteen Rods to a Stake and Stones—thence southerly nineteen Rods and a half by the Fence to the first mentioned Bounds—and contains seventeen Acres and Sixty one Rods—We appraise said Piece of Land at one hundred and eighty two dollars and thirty seven cents—and we do award that the said Jerusha pay her Sister Sarah Osgood twenty one Dollars and twenty Cents and that she pay her Sister Amie Young fifteen Dollars and thirty Cents—which Land as above described we do assign to the said Jerusha as the whole of her share in the said Israel's Estate.

Secondly, assigned to Submit Cummins Daughter to Israel Standish the following Piece of Land being Part of said Israel's Homestead which is bounded as follows Beginning at the Northwest Corner of the said Jerusha Spinnage's Lane as above described thence North seven Degrees thirty three Rods and sixteen Links to a Stake and Stones (blurred) . . . to he said Submit as her Share in the Estate.

Chapter Twenty-two

FINDING CAPTAIN MYLES STANDISH

Finding Amie and Submit

Thirdly, we have assigned to Elizabeth Loomis, Daughter of the said Israel Standish the following Piece of Land beginning at the North East Corner of the said Submit Cummins' Land as above said hence South ten Degrees West twenty Rods to a Stake and Stones—thence south three Degrees East fifty three Rods to a Stake and Stones—thence East thirteen Degrees South nineteen rods to a Stake and Stones—thence North eighteen Degrees East seventy one Rods to a Stake and Stones—thence West eighteen Degrees North Forty Rods and an half to the first mentioned Bounds and contains fourteen Acres and three Rods and was appraised at one hundred thirty three Dollars and eight Cents.

The above Land and the Money the said Elizabeth is to receive from her Sister Submit Cummins we do assign to her as her whole share in said Estate. Fourthly, we have assigned to Sarah Osgood Daughter to the said Israel Standish the following Piece of Orchard, Viz:

Beginning at the North West Corner of the widow Sarah Standishe's Land thence Easterly by sixteen Rods and fifteen Links to a Stake and Stones—thence Northerly by the Widow Sarah Standishe's Land thirteen Rods and a Quarter to a Stake and Stones—thence West fourteen Degrees North eighteen Rods and eighteen Links to a Stake and Stones. In the Line of Roger Brunson's Land thence Southerly by said Brunson's Land thirteen Rods and was appraised at one hundred and twenty four Dollars which Land with the Money she is to receive from her sister Jerusha Spinnage.

Fifthly, assigned to Amie Young Daughter to the said Israel Standish the following Piece of Orchard, Viz. Beginning at the North West corner of the said Sarah Osgood's Land as described thence East fourteen Degrees South eighteen Rods and eighteen Links to a Stake and Stones—thence Northerly by the Widow Sarah Standishe's Land thirteen Rods and a Quarter to a Stake and Stones in Widow Sarah Standishe's line—thence Westerly by said Standishe's Land eighteen Rods to Roger Brunson's Land thence Southerly by said Land thirteen Rods to the first mentioned Bounds and contains one acre and seventy Rods . . . appraised at one hundred and twenty seven Dollars . . . and two ninth Parts of a Pew in the Baptist Meeting House formerly owned by said Standish-which with the Money she is to receive from her Sister Jerusha Spinnage and Submit Cummins. We have assigned to her as the whole of her Share of said Estate.

Chapter Twenty-two

FINDING CAPTAIN MYLES STANDISH

Finding Amie and Submit

In Witness whereof we have hereunto set our Hands this twenty seventh day of May in the year of our Lord one thousand eight hundred and six.

John Looms (for Elizabeth)	*Witness:*
Amie Young	
Bezin Benton Agent for	*Henry Basset*
Daniel Spinnage (for Jerusha Standish)	*John Alden*
Jonathan	*Ebenr Smith*
Cummins (for Submit)	
Eliah Lilly attorney (for Sarah) Osgood	

Hampshire, ss.   Northampton, Mass., November 23, 1948

October 15, 1824   Franklin County Land Record 108:24:

  Amie Young of Conway sells to Enos Harvey. . . "A certain parcel of land or orchard being the north part of the original orchard of Israel Standish deceased, and bounded & lying as follows in Ashfield, County of Franklin, Commonwealth aforesaid & bounded South by orchard owned by Enos Harvey on East & North by the dower set off to the widow of the aforementioned Israel Standish, deceased, in West by land owned by Moses Sims, being all the share or part of the real estate of Israel Standish, deceased, which was set off to me this Amie Young, the youngest heir of the above deceased, supposed to contain about one acre and three quarters, be the same more or less." Signed, sealed and delivered in the presence of "Amy Young."

  Witnessed by: *Alonzo Young, Sorphena (sp) Harvey, Lydia Harvey*

Chapter Twenty-two

FINDING CAPTAIN MYLES STANDISH

Finding Amie and Submit

Amie apparently retained ownership of her portion of her father's twenty-seven acre orchard until 1824 when she sold it to Enos Harvey. He was the son of the widow Sarah Harvey, a next-door neighbor who became Israel's second wife in 1794.

Almost nothing is known about Amie's husband, John Young. The fact that she signed Israel's probate record in her own right, suggests that by 1806 she and John were separated, divorced, or that he had died. Where and when he was born, married and died remains a mystery, but there may be a simple explanation for this. I now think it is quite possible, even likely, that John and Amie's record of marriage, children's birth, property purchase, etc., was destroyed by the burning of the Conway Town hall; it would explain why the two of them are "non-persons." The same may be true for Submit and Jonathan Cummings. Family lore says John Young's father was a Methodist minister who served as chaplain with General Washington's army during the terrible Valley Forge winter where he suffered severe frostbite. I am unable to find a record of his war service due to the commonality of his last name and the fact that I do not know his first name. My undocumented reference for him is another previously mentioned Young family researcher, Ione Cumberland, now deceased.

Chapter Twenty-three

FINDING CAPTAIN MYLES STANDISH

Genealogic Jig Saw Puzzle

On the long drive back to Wisconsin, we reflected upon all the wonderful people who had been helpful to us along the way. We began with many pieces still missing from our genealogic jigsaw puzzle and finished up with all of them neatly in place.

Over a period of many months, I had written to dozens of County Clerks, Register of Deeds and appropriate historical societies in every county seat where I had established or suspected that our ancestors had once lived. This advanced spadework, plus our "office coffee fund" concept enabled us to recruit a cadre of critically placed folks willing to go the extra mile on our behalf.

The normal record "look-up" process was pretty much the same for every county office we contacted. Once a letter of inquiry was received by them and the requested information located, a form letter was sent back to the requestor advising that a copy of the sought after document would be sent as soon as the necessary ten or fifteen-dollar service fee was received. Over time, I learned from the responding clerks that, quite often the requestor failed to respond, or even more aggravating, attempted to negotiate the service fee. After discovering this, I made it a practice to include a twenty-dollar check with my original search request along with a note that read, "If there is any excess please do not send a refund but consider it as a thank you contribution to your office coffee fund."

Not only were my search requests returned to me much more promptly, but also a handwritten thank you note was often included with the documents. More than once, after the particular record I asked for could not be found, the clerk continued to search for some other type of document under the same person's name and forwarded a copy of, say, a land purchase record I never would have thought to ask for. This is exactly the kind of breakthrough we experienced at the Franklin County Court House; the birth record was not there, but Amie's father's probate record was and it contained the information I needed.

Chapter Twenty-three

FINDING CAPTAIN MYLES STANDISH

Genealogic Jig Saw Puzzle

Why had it been so difficult to prove Amie's parentage, even her existence? There were several likely causes for this, the primary one being that for some unexplained reason, she and her next oldest sister, Submit, had never been listed in Ashfield Vital Records; not their births, marriages, children, nothing.

This omission had not been the case with Israel's four older children, those born prior to 1773. This fact made it all the more puzzling; one would expect Ashfield Births to list them all or none. Instead, we now knew it had been only Israel's two youngest children that were excluded. Had Israel perhaps been among those who followed the "peppermint trade" to the state of New York and Submit and Amie were born there? There is no evidence of this, however. When his first wife Elizabeth died in 1792, he was still living at Baptist Corners and married the Widow Harvey, a next-door neighbor, two years later when Amie would have been age twelve. Was it possible that both girls had been placed for adoption or taken in by an older sibling or other relative?

It is understandable that Ada Ball Cass, an earlier Young family researcher was stymied at this point. Family lore was sufficient for her to "know" ancestor John Young had married a descendant of Captain Myles Standish but she and other researchers had been unable to document the connection. I, on the other hand, had been fortunate in having the assistance of Elaine Corbett of the Duxbury Pilgrim Society and all the advice and resources she had to offer.

But in the end, it was the helpful assistant at the office of the Franklin County Register of Deeds that made the critical difference. I regret that, after some 18 years I cannot recall her name and my notes of that particular visit cannot be found.

Nor have I been able to discover what happened to Submit in her adulthood. She was age 28-29 when she received her share of her father's estate. Her husband, Jonathan Cummings, signed the document on her behalf, as was the custom in those days. John Loomis signed for his wife, Elizabeth. Agent Bezin Benton signed in place of Jerusha's husband, Daniel Spinnage and Sarah Standish Osgood was represented by attorney Eliah Lilly. Amie was age 25-26, the mother of two small children and supposedly married to John Young but, unlike her sisters; she signed the probate document for herself, indicating that John was either deceased or simply no longer in the picture.

It has been suggested that John was born in Rhode Island but obtaining further information about a man with such a common name whose exact birth date and place is unknown within that state, is quite impossible, there being so many hundreds of them. Perhaps someone else will have better luck; I certainly hope so.

Chapter Twenty-three

FINDING CAPTAIN MYLES STANDISH

Genealogic Jig Saw Puzzle

Upon returning home, I wrote to thank Mrs. Harris once again for her many courtesies and told her of our visit to the office of the Franklin County Register of Deeds and how, thanks to a helpful clerk, we found Amie and Submit listed among the Israel Standish heirs in his probate records.

Along with her congratulations, Mrs. Harris added that there were a number of other such inconsistencies in the Ashfield records due to the fact that they had been compiled from the original documents by volunteers many years after the fact and, due to the age and condition of the originals, many such errors resulted.

This bit of information was more than a little surprising to us; the copy of the Standish section of the Ashfield Vital Records that had been sent to us looked, for all the world, like original, official documents; the final word, so to speak.

In hindsight, we undoubtedly would have been aware of such a possibility had we received the entire book and been able to read the introductory preface, but the selected pages sent to us pertained to the Standish family only and lacked this critical bit of introductory information.

Even though we had experienced similar mistakes in ancestral birth and death records with other ancestral searches, such a simple explanation for Amie's omission had never occurred to us. As Mrs. Harris wrote, "I agree that the children of Israel Standish must have had Elizabeth (not Sarah) for a mother and that when these birth records were complied he was by then married to Sara", (The Widow Sarah Harvey). "Stranger things have happened as recorded in the Vital Records. One man had 15 children and their mother was recorded as Anne and Chloe. I also found six children recorded for one date, and certainly not multiple births!"

So, at long last, the missing Amie mystery was solved to our considerable satisfaction. We were indeed descended from the famous Captain Standish. Grandmother Victoria was right all along.

Knowing that the Mayflower Society was about to publish "Mayflower Families in Progress (MFFIP), Myles Standish, 5 Generations," I sent them copies of Israel's probate record. I was pleased to have them accept it as verification of the names of Israel Standish's children. Amie is now properly listed as a descendant of Captain Myles Standish, his 3rd great granddaughter. This pamphlet is available for about ten dollars directly from the Mayflower Society, 4 Winslow Street, Plymouth, MA 02361.

Richard Hafeman Haviland   March 2009

Chapter Twenty-four

FINDING CAPTAIN MYLES STANDISH

The Standish-Young Lineage

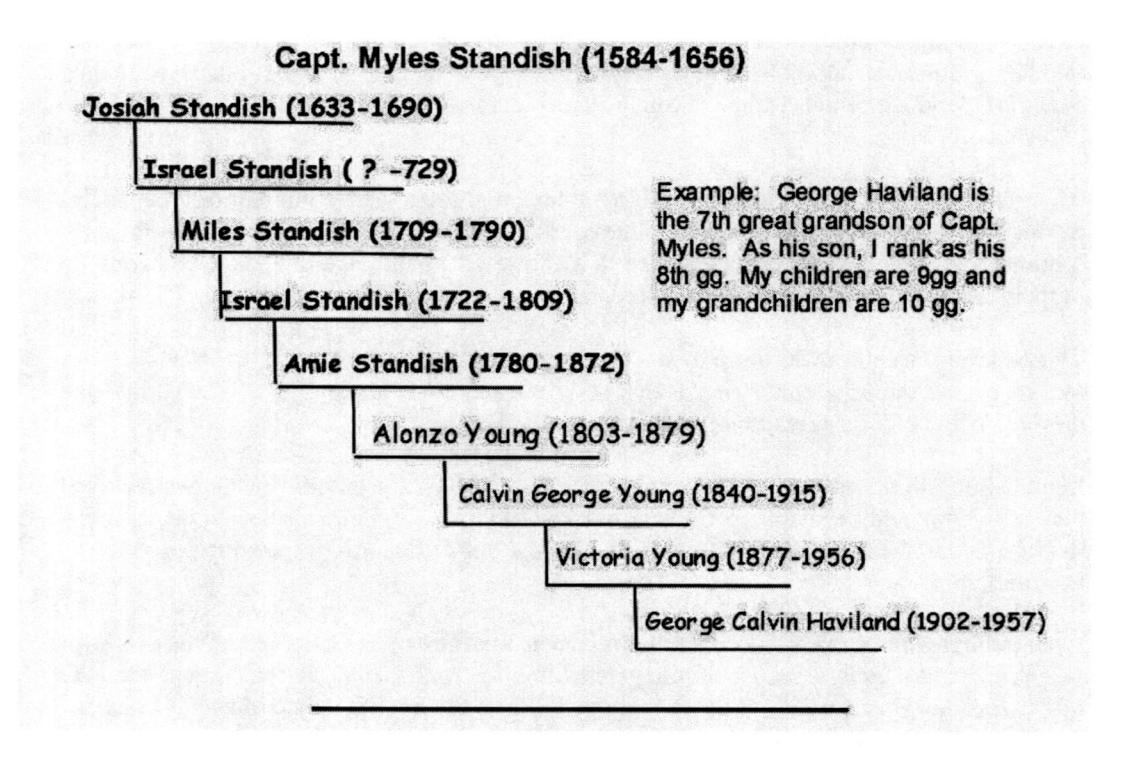

```
Capt. Myles Standish (1584-1656)
 └─ Josiah Standish (1633-1690)
     └─ Israel Standish ( ? -729)
         └─ Miles Standish (1709-1790)
             └─ Israel Standish (1722-1809)
                 └─ Amie Standish (1780-1872)
                     └─ Alonzo Young (1803-1879)
                         └─ Calvin George Young (1840-1915)
                             └─ Victoria Young (1877-1956)
                                 └─ George Calvin Haviland (1902-1957)
```

Example: George Haviland is the 7th great grandson of Capt. Myles. As his son, I rank as his 8th gg. My children are 9gg and my grandchildren are 10 gg.

At first glance, ancestor charts can sometimes be confusing to the uninitiated. For that reason, the above diagram is designed to help clarify the relationship of the alpha ancestor (Myles Standish) to his interested descendants. This chart is limited to just names, birth and death dates of line ancestors only. Captain Myles, for example, had a total of seven children but his fifth son, Josiah, is the only one included here since he is a direct-line family ancestor. The chart also includes the next four generations of Amie Standish's progeny, these names irregular, non-bold type.

Following these paragraphs, the reader will find much more detailed information about the same ancestors, but again, siblings are not included for reasons of simplicity. However, complete Standish-Young-Haviland lineage with all siblings and their children included for each generation is available from the author at moderate cost. They contain informative editorial comments and are quite lengthy, running to more than 50 pages. Lest anyone reading this begins to feel overly important by virtue of being a descendant of the famous captain, there are a great many others. A 1958 estimate by a Mayflower researcher put the total at well over 5,000. By now, it must be at least double or triple that.

Chapter Twenty-four

FINDING CAPTAIN MYLES STANDISH

The Standish-Young Lineage

CAPTAIN MYLES STANDISH
EIGHT GENERATIONS

Capt. Myles Standish
        b. 1584 d. 3 Oct 1656
        m 1, Rose d. 29 Jan 1621
        m 2, Barbara m. Aug 1623 d. aft. 6 Oct 1659

Before he was age twenty, Lieutenant Myles Standish was sent to Holland by Queen Elizabeth as part of a 5,000 man army to prevent Spanish King Phillip from making that country a Catholic nation from which he could more easily assault England. Severely wounded in the 1603 Battle of Ostend, Myles remained in Holland, probably on occupation duty, for some fifteen years. During this time, he met and married Rose, her last name unknown. He became friends with John Robinson, pastor of the English congregation that had recently relocated to Holland. Robinson asked Myles to serve as their military advisor on their upcoming Virginia colonization project.

Second Generation

Josiah Standish   b. c. 1633 d. 19 Mar 1690

b. c. 1633 in Duxbury, MA. He married (1) Mary Dingley, married 19 Dec 1654 in Marshfield, MA, (daughter of John Dingley and Sarah ___) d. 1 Jul 1655 in Duxbury, MA. He married (2) Sarah Allen, married aft 7 Mar 1654 in Marshfield, MA, b. 30 Mar 1639, (daughter of Samuel Allen and Ann Whitemore) d. aft Sep 1690. Josiah died 19 Mar 1690 in Preston, CT. Josiah was Lieutenant of Bridgewater Militia, 1660. Elected Duxburrow Selectman by 1666. Frequently elected Deputy of Plymouth Colony. Moved to Norwich, Ct, and held rank of Captain by 1686. On 5 Feb 1686, now of Norwich, he purchased 150 acres from John Parks. He spent the last years of his life in Preston, CT, dying there about age 57. Ref: MFFIP, Standish, Five Gen, p. 4.

Third Generation

Israel (1) Standish
        b. bef. Jan 1729 in Duxbury, MA
        m. 8 Feb 1703 Elizabeth Richards, OF Preston, CT
        d. bef. Jan 172, Preston, CT

Chapter Twenty-four

FINDING CAPTAIN MYLES STANDISH

The Standish-Young Lineage

Fourth Generation

Miles Standish
    b. 18 Nov 1709 in Preston, CT,
    m. (1) Jerusha Fuller, 2 Nov 1737 in Mansfield, CT,
    m. (2) Hannah _____, in Ashfield, MA.
    m. (3) Mehetabel Orcut, 21 Apr 1773 in Ashfield, MA.
    Miles died aft. 1790 in Ashfield, MA.

Moved first to Stafford, Ct. prior to 1738 when he signed Baptist church documents there. He next bought Mansfield Hollow property but sold it back to the former owner shortly after birth of his first child, Israel. Later bought land in "Baptist Corners" near Ashfield from a John Alden. Tax rolls show joint ownership with son Israel. About 1768, Miles helped build the Baptist Corners Church.

Fifth Generation

Israel (2) Standish
    b. 22 Apr 1738 in Mansfield, CT.
    m. (1) Sarah Patrick, of Ashfiled MA.
    m. ed (2) Sarah Harvey, Nov 1794 of Ashfield, MA.
    Israel died Aug 1804 in Ashfield, MA.

Sixth Generation

Amie Standish
    b. 8 Sep 1780 In Ashfield, MA
    m. ab 1802 ?, location unknown
    d. 1872 ? Erie Co, PA?

As explained in the preceding chapters of "Finding Captain Myles Standish," Amie (Amy) Standish, through no fault of her own, has been one of the most elusive ancestors to research.

Chapter Twenty-four

FINDING CAPTAIN MYLES STANDISH

The Standish-Young Lineage

Seventh Generation

Alonzo Young

    b. 14 Apr 1803 – d. 9 May 1879
    m. (1) Seloma Loomis
    m. (2) Mary Ann Holcomb

Alonzo lived in Erie County's Wayne Twp before moving to Amity Twp, also in Erie Co PA. Eldest daughters Esther & Amy were quite small when first wife, Seloma, died. After he married Mary Ann Holcomb, Alonzo bought farm property from Merrill Lomis, his former father-in-law, where he built a log cabin and sired nine additional children.

Eighth Generation

Calvin George Young

    b, 1820 Apr 1845   Amity Twp. Erie Co, PA
    m. 6 Feb. 1872   De Pere, WI
    d. 15 Oct 1915, Bryant, WI

Shortly before Christmas, 1863, Calvin, then age 23, enlisted in the 125th Ohio Volunteers. The 125th participated in Sherman's famous "March to the Sea," and fought in a series of extremely bloody battles all across Georgia: Rocky Face Ridge; Resaca; New Hope Church; Kennesaw Mountain; Big Shanty and Peach Tree Creek as well as the siege of Atlanta. When the regiment was mustered out of service at Ft. Irwin, Texas, on the 25th of September, 1865, Calvin was in an army hospital, although apparently unwounded, there being no mention of him suffering wounds in his service records.

Ninth Generation

Victoria Young

    b. 8 Apr 1877   Deere, WI
    m. 25 May 1894   Antigo, WI (Langlade Co. Marriages, Vol I, p.104.)
    d. 5 Nov 1956 Bryant, WI (Langlade Co. Death Register, V.16, p.131.)

Chapter Twenty-four

FINDING CAPTAIN MYLES STANDISH

The Standish-Young Lineage

In 1881, four-year old Victoria and her parents were aboard the very first passenger train to pull into the booming new city of Antigo, already grown to nearly 3,000. Tory had just turned seventeen when she married Andrew Haviland, a logger at the camp where Tory and her mother, Mathilda, were the camp cooks. It was not a successful union, however. After fathering five children, Andrew left his family and went back to Michigan.

Tenth Generation

George Calvin Haviland
   b. 16 Apr 1902   Antigo, WI
   m. 8 Aug 1931   ?
   d. 28 Nov 1957   La Crosse, WI

Although his birth record is unrecorded in the Langlade Co. Birth Register, his sister Blanche says there is no doubt but that he was born there. George farmed in Langlade Co. for 17 yrs prior to his divorce. He remarried in La Crosse, WI, became Maintenance Superintendent of the La Crosse St. Joseph hospital.

The first half dozen ancestors listed in the foregoing descendancy chart have been taken directly from the 1990 publication," Myles Standish of the Mayflower and His Descendants for Five Generations." Compiled by Russell L. Warner, it can be ordered directly from the Mayflower Society, 4 Winslow St, Plymouth, MA 02361. The price is less than ten dollars.

It is fair to say that Amie Standish would almost certainly have been omitted had I not been able to send Mr. Warner documentation proving that she and her sister, Submit, are entitled to be listed as Israel's children. My contribution was kindly acknowledged by Mr. Warner, giving me no little degree of satisfaction.

Chapter Twenty-five

FINDING CAPTAIN MYLES STANDISH

A Frequently Asked Question

"How many ancestors does someone like me have in my family tree?"

Actually, we all have the same number of them, depending on how many generations back one wants to go. In any case, it turns out to be lot more than most people think. We may not know their names, but go back far enough and we all have millions of them. Chances are that some of them are famous, some of them infamous. One of the advantages of researching a famous ancestor is that it is much easier to find vital records for that person and his or her descendants.

Even though we probably do not know the names of most of them, our ancestors, famous or infamous, make us what we are. Except for our grandparents, they never heard of us either, but their genes contribute to our brainpower, how we think and act and how we look; something to think about the next time you look upon an old family photograph.

Chapter Twenty-five

FINDING CAPTAIN MYLES STANDISH

A Frequently Asked Question

Gen	Added Gr-Parents	Total number of Ancestors
1	0	Just you
2	2	2 parents
3	6	2 parents + 4 g-parents
4	14	(2 parents + 4 g-parents + 8 g-grandparents)
5	30	(2 parents + 4 g-parents + 16 g-grandparents)
6	62	(2 parents + 4 g-parents + 32 g-grandparents)
7	126	(2 parents + 4 g-parents + 64 g-grandparents)
8	254	(2 parents + 4 g-parents + 128 g-grandparents)

The above chart illustrates how many we all have in just our last eight generations—the same number of generations it takes to get from Captain Myles Standish down to Grandmother Tory. For those who like playing with numbers, see for yourself how many generations it takes to reach a million.

The information shown here regarding Myles Standish's ancestry is taken from G.V.C. Young's 1983 work which makes a strong case for Myles being born and raised on the Isle of Man, just off the western coast of England. (See bibliography reference # 10, 11, 12).

Chapter Twenty-five

FINDING CAPTAIN MYLES STANDISH

A Frequently Asked Question

Known Ancestors of Captain Myles Standish

Myles Standish Capt., b. 1584 in Ellanbane, Isle of Man, d. 3 Oct 1656 in Duxbury, MA.

He married (1) Rose _____, b. in England, d. 29 Jan 1621 in Plymouth, MA.

He married (2) Barbara ____, married Aug 1623 in Plymouth, MA, d. aft. 6 Oct 1659 in Duxbury, MA.

Parents

2. **John Standish Jr.**, b. in Isle of Man, England, d. Dec 1601 in Isle of Man, England. He married Alice Lace.

3. **Alice Lace**, b. in Isle of Man? d. 1608 in Isle of Man.

Grandparents

4. **John Standish Sr.**, b. in Isle of Man, England, d. 1602 in Isle of Man, England. He married (1) Mallie Moore Gilbert, d. 1618. He married (2) Christian Lace.

5. **Mallie Moore Gilbert**, d. 1618.

Great Grandparents

8. **Huan Standish**, b. in Isle of Man, England?.

Great Great Grandparents

16. **Robert Standish**, b. bef.1502 in Ormskirk, Lancashire, England, d. aft.1529. He married Margaret Croft.

17. **Margaret Croft**.

Chapter Twenty-five

FINDING CAPTAIN MYLES STANDISH

A Frequently Asked Question

3rd Great Grandparents

32. **Gilbert Standish,** b. in Ormskirk, Lancashire, England.

4th Great Grandparents

64. **Hugh Standish II.**

5th Great Grandparents

128. **William Standish,** b. in Ormskirk, Lancashire, England.

6th Great Grandparents

256. **John II Standish.**

7th Great Grandparents

512. **Ralph Standish, Sir,** b. c. 1382 in Isle of Man, England? He married Mary De Ince.

513. **Mary De Ince.**

8th Great Grandparents

1024. **John I De Standish,** b. c. 1353 in Isle of Man ENG (?). He married Margaret _____.

1025. **Margaret _____.**

Chapter Twenty-six

FINDING CAPTAIN MYLES STANDISH

BIBLIOGRAHY

1. STANDISH MONUMENT EXERCISES OF CONSECRATION

    Duxbury, Aug. 17, 1871

    Prepared by Stephen M. Allen Corresponding Secretary

    of the Standish Monument Association

    Alfred Mudge & Son, Printers, Boston MA

2. HISTORY OF PLIMOUTH PLANTATION

    William Bradford, Second Governor of the Colony

    From the Original Manuscript

    for The Massachusetts Historical Society. Boston, MA 1856

    Little, Brown & Company, Publishers

3. BRADFORD'S HISTORY OF PLYMOUTH PLANTATION 1606 - 1646

    Edited by William T Davis, Pres. of the Pilgrim Society   1908

    Chas. Scribner's Sons, New York.

4. THE PILGRIMS: THEIR JOURNEYS & THEIR WORLD

    Francis Dillion   1975

    Doubleday & Co, Inc. Garden City, New York

5. WEBSTER'S AMERICAN BIOGRAPIES

    Chas Van Doren, Editor 1975

    G. & C. Merriam Company, Publishers   Springfield, MA.

Chapter Twenty-six

LOOKING FOR CAPTAIN MYLES STANDISH

BIBLIOGRAHY

6. THE PILGRIMS AND THEIR HISTORY
   Roland G Usher, Ph.D.   1977
   Corner House Publishers   Williamstown, MA

7. HIISTORY OF PLIMOUTH PLANTATION   1620 - 1747
   William Bradford
   Edited by Samuel Eliot Morison   1963
   Alfred A. Knopf New York,

8. ELIZABETH THE GREAT
   Elizabeth Jenkins   1958
   Coward-McCann, Inc   New York

9. HOMES IN THE WILDERNESS
   William Bradford and Others of the Mayflower Company
   Margaret Wise Brown, Editor 1968
   Limmet Books: Hamden, Connecticut

10. PILGRIM MYLES STANDISH, First Manx-American
    G.V.C. YOUNG   1984
    The Mansk-Svenska Publishing Co   Isle of Man

11. MORE ABOUT PILGRIM MYLES STANDISH
    G.V.C YOUNG   1987
    The Mansk-Svenska Publishing Co   Isle of Man

Chapter Twenty-six

FINDING CAPTAIN MYLES STANDISH

BIBLIOGRAHY

12. ELLANBANE WAS THE BIRTHPLACE OF MYLES STANDISH

    G.V.C. YOUNG   1988

    The Mansk-Svenska Publishing Co   Isle of Man

13. ARMS & ARMOR of the PILGRIMS

    Harold L. Peterson   1957

    Plymouth Plantation & the Pilgrim Society Plymouth MA

14. MORT'S RELATION

    Nathaniel Morton

    (The earliest published account of Plymouth Colony, 1622).

15. MYLES STANDISH of the MAYFLOWER

    And his Descendants for Five Generations

    Complied by Russell L. Warner

    Edited by Robert S. Wakefied FASG

    Published by General Society of Mayflower Descendants, 1990

16. LISTEN TO THE ECHOES

    Roberta K. Smith

    The Mansfield Historical Society   (1983)

17. COUNTY SEATS LISTED BY STATES:

    Note: Most public reference libraries can furnish this, but the best way now to get this information is to do an online "Google Search:" <u>County seats by States</u>.